LONG ISLAND
UNIVERSITY
LIBRARIES

THE POWER OF STORY

· ·

TEACHING THROUGH STORYTELLING

SECOND EDITION

D0164800

DISCARDED
FROM
LIU LIBRARIES

INSTRUCTIONAL

IMc MEDIA CENTER

C.W. POST CAMPUS OF L.I.U.

TEACHER'S COPY
DO NOT CIRCULATE

THE POWER OF STORY

TEACHING THROUGH STORYTELLING

SECOND EDITION

Rives Collins
Northwestern University

Pamela J. Cooper
Northwestern University

Allyn and Bacon

Boston • London • Toronto • Sydney • Tokyo • Singapore

Publisher:	Gay L. Pauley
Editor:	A. Colette Kelly
Developmental Editor:	Katie E. Bradford
Production Editor:	Ann Waggoner Aken
Cover Design:	Don Giannatti
Typesetting:	Andrea Reider

Copyright © 1997 by Allyn & Bacon
A Viacom Company
160 Gould Street
Needham Heights, MA 02194

Internet: www.abacon.com
America Online: keyword: College Online

10 9 8 7 6 5 4

All rights reserved. No part of this publication may be reproduced, stored in a retrieval system, or transmitted in any form or by any means, electronic, mechanical, photocopy, recording, or otherwise, without the prior written permission of the publisher.

Excerpt from THE LITTLE PRINCE by Antoine de Saint-Exupery, copyright 1943 and renewed 1971 by Harcourt Brace & Company, reprinted by permission of the publisher.

Printed in the United States of America

Library of Congress Cataloging-in-Publication Data

Collins, Rives.
      The power of story : teaching through storytelling / by Rives Collins, Pamela J. Cooper.—2nd ed.
            p.   cm.
      Rev. ed. of : Look what happened to Frog / Pamela J. Cooper, Rives Collins.
      Includes bibliographical references.
      ISBN 0-13776-709-9
      1. Storytelling.   2. Activity programs in education.   3. Oral reading.
I. Cooper, Pamela J. II. Cooper, Pamela J. Look what happened to Frog.
III. Title.
LB1042.C488   1997
372.64'2—dc20   96-25417
                                                                              CIP

Contents

IMC
REF.
LB
1042
.C488
1997

List of Activities Found in Chapter 8*

* (Activity title and page number)

Preface

We'll begin with a poem about stories:

WHY WE TELL STORIES

for Linda Foster

1

Because we used to have leaves
and on damp days
our muscles feel a tug, painful now, from when roots pulled us into
    the ground

and because our children believe they can fly, an instinct retained from
    when the
bones in our arms
were shaped like zithers and broke neatly under their feathers

and because before we had lungs
we know how far it was to the bottom
as we floated open-eyed
like painted scarves through the scenery
of dreams, and because we awakened

and learned to speak

2

We sat by the fire in our caves,
and because we were poor, we made up a tale
about a treasure mountain
that would open only for us

and because we were always defeated,
we invented impossible riddles
only we could solve,
monsters only we could kill,
women who could love no one else

and because we had survived
sisters and brother, daughters and sons,
we discovered bones that rose
from the dark earth and sang
as white birds in the trees

3

Because the story of our life
becomes our life

Because each of us tells
the same story
but tells it differently

and none of us tells it
the same way twice

Because grandmothers looking like spiders
want to enchant the children
and grandfathers need to convince us
what happened because of them

and though we listen only
haphazardly, with one ear,
we will begin our story
with the word and

—*Lisel Mueller*

We wrote this book, in part, because we wanted to explore why we tell stories. We wrote the book also because we love to tell stories, because we believe they are the part of us that makes us human, and because we believe they are at the heart of the teaching/learning process.

There are changes to this second edition. We have added more profiles of storytellers as well as some new activities and resources. We've also added a new chapter on family stories, "We All Have Stories." These additions reflect our view that family stories are at the heart of each of our personal identities and are at the core of the current storytelling revival.

As you read this book, please be aware of the following styles and treatments. First, we have chosen not to use the awkward construction "he/she." Instead, we have used "he" and "she" alternately throughout the text, as a more comfortable means of avoiding sexist language. Second, we have chosen to write the book in the first person singular, even though this is a co-authored book. Because each of us contributed several personal stories and examples, using "I" rather than "we" was simpler and clearer. Third, this book is highly personal. Much of what we have written comes from our own personal experience in storytelling, in teaching storytelling, and in using storytelling in our teaching. What you will read are guidelines, ideas we have found to work. Because storytelling is so personal, you will find your own ways of telling and using stories. Finally, we make use of many stories to teach storytelling, both our own and the stories of others.

The first two chapters answer the question, "Why should I tell stories?" The next five chapters answer the question, "How do I tell stories?" The final chapter provides several storytelling activities that we have found work well in our classrooms and storytelling workshops.

In addition to the why, how, and activities, we've included numerous resources—both print and nonprint. We have also included a feature, "Meet the Storyteller,"—interviews with people who use storytelling a great deal in their own lives and/or in their professions.

The storytellers profiled here represent a variety of storytelling voices and styles, yet all are successful. They range in age from four years old to "retirement age." They include children, professional storytellers, classroom teachers, librarians, and drama specialists. They all speak to the "joy of story" and the fact that we are all storytellers.

Because our own stories are inescapably entwined with the stories of others, we are indebted to many people. Our students have taught us much. This book is, in a very real sense, their story. The reviewers of this text—Bob Cocetti, Arlie Daniel, and Debbie Simon—helped us "fine tune" the story, as did Colette Kelly, our editor.

We thank Dawn Murray, our photographer, who tells stories with her camera. Susan Zeder and Jim Hancock's "Inner Sources" writing workshop was invaluable to us in helping us find our own voices. Master storytellers Donald Doyle, Jay O'Callahan, Lynn Rubright, and Donald Davis have taught and performed brilliantly on our campus; we are grateful for the excellence of their examples. Thanks also to Carlyn Armintrout, who made sense of our scratches and typed the final manuscript.

Finally, our families continue to furnish the time, space, and unconditional love that gave us the confidence to tell the story.

"Why We Tell Stories," reprinted by permission of Louisiana State University Press from *The Need to Hold Still* by Lisel Mueller. Copyright © 1980 by Lisel Mueller.

To the ones who are at the center
of our stories—
Rick, Jamie, Jenifer, Bryan,
Kirsty, Caitlin, and Ethan

And to Donald P. Doyle,
Professor Emeritus of Theatre
at Arizona State University,
who reminds us that teaching is an art form
and who tells stories
as if our lives depended on them.

CHAPTER 1

••••••••••••••••••••

Storytelling Is...

The telling of a tale links you with everyone who has told it before. There are no new tales, only new tellers in their own way, and if you listen closely you can hear the voice of everyone who ever told the tale.

William Brooke

LEWIS CARROLL once called stories "love gifts." Indeed, when we tell stories, we do give a gift. Storytelling creates for our listeners a sense of mystery, of wonder, of reverence for life. Perhaps most important, storytelling creates a relationship. When I ask my students about their experiences with storytelling, they often remember the closeness, the sharing, but may not remember the actual stories! One student remarked: "I don't remember what stories my father told me. I only remember that storytelling created a special bond between us. It wasn't what he told. It was the wonderful knowledge that he found me important enough to take time to tell stories to me." I asked my then seven-year-old daughter, Jamie, "What would the world be like if there were no stories?" She replied, "Dull, boring, and nothing to say."

Some storytellers work a quiet, special magic; some, a raucous magic. They are at once the weavers of fantasy, the keepers of genealogies, the keepers of history, wits, wisdom-sayers, spinners of ideas. Storytelling is an art, a science, a way of life. To define storytelling or storyteller is to try to make concrete that which is abstract. Suffice it to say that storytelling is among the oldest forms of communication. It exists in every culture. Storytelling is the commonality of all human beings, in all places, in all times. It is used to educate, to inspire, to record historical events, to entertain, to transmit cultural mores.

Storytellers are...

Who are the storytellers? Well, in a general sense, we all are. As my daughter Jamie says, "Everything you tell is a story." If that is true (and I believe it is), storytelling becomes a vehicle for discovering who we are, for making sense of our world, for enhancing our learning/teaching, and for plain old fun!

In his book *Human Communication as Narration: Toward a Philosophy of Reason, Value, and Action,* Fisher (1989) suggests that human beings are inherently storytellers. Humans experience and understand life as a "series of ongoing narratives, as conflicts, characters, beginnings, middles, and ends" (p. 24). Thus all forms of communication can be seen fundamentally as stories—symbolic interpretations of aspects of the world occurring in time and shaped by history, culture, and character. McAdams (1993) suggests: "We are all tellers of tales. We each seek to provide our scattered and often confusing experiences with a sense of coherence by arranging the episodes of our lives into stories" (p. 11).

Although in a general sense all humans are storytellers, some humans have chosen to use story for specific purposes: for teaching, as oral history, for entertainment, for healing, and for sacred rites. Throughout history, special individuals have acted as keepers and tellers of stories. The ollahms and shanachies of Ireland, the griots of Africa, the Navajo shaman, the troubadours of medieval France—these were the storytellers of old who held honored places in their particular societies. Though none of us may achieve the artistry of these masters whose lives were devoted to storytelling, it is their family that I invite you to join. I encourage you to step into the ancient shoes of the teacher-tellers, to become the "givers and interpreters of myth." Whether you teach first graders or tenth graders, I encourage you to become a teacher-teller and, in turn, to encourage your students to become teacher-tellers. Why? Because, it seems to me, story is at the very heart of teaching and learning.

Stories are …

Livo and Rietz (1986) explain that " 'Story' is a universal mirror that shows us the 'truth' about ourselves—who and why we are. When we look into this mirror, we see daily routine and mundane circumstances transformed into something profound. 'Story' takes the ordinary and binds it into all of human existence, revealing the significance of the trivial" (p. 4).

Schoafsma (1989) suggests that stories may be seen as *selves*, provisional representations of our struggle to define ourselves and the world. But in the process of shaping those selves, stories also may become one means of shaping relationships with others in the community. In the words of Bruner (1986), a story provides a "map of possible roles and possible worlds in which action, thought, and self-definition are possible (or desirable)" (p. 66). Students, through their stories, explore personal "roles" and "possible worlds." Sit in a preschool classroom, or listen to the play of elementary-school children or the conversations of adolescents. Words you will hear are, "Let's pretend that…" and "What if…" Words like these signal a "trying on" of roles, an exploration of whether they are viable or workable.

The power of story

Storytelling is a powerful teaching/learning tool. In her book *The Boy Who Would Be a Helicopter*, Vivian Paley (1990) tells why story is so important to teaching:

> A day without storytelling is, for me, a disconnected day. The children at least have their play, but I cannot remember what is real to the children without their stories to anchor fantasy and purpose. (p. 4)

By listening to our students, we as teachers can learn what is real to them, and thus know what questions to ask and comments to make to enhance their learning.

For example, when Jamie was six, we had a conversation about how sweets could turn teeth yellow. I was trying to impress upon her the importance of (a) not eating a lot of sweets, and (b) brushing her teeth. Later that day, she dictated the following three stories:

THREE-EYEBALLED MONSTER WITH A YELLOW SMILE

The three-eyeballed monster with a yellow smile eats sweets. It's eight feet tall. It eats ten sweets a day. Its favorite sweets are *all* sweets. That's why he has a yellow smile.

THE END

THE SILLYRAMJUICE MONSTER

The Sillyramjuice Monster eats three houses a day because it has three heads. Its favorite game is eating houses. It is thirteen feet tall. It drinks lakes. It likes all the toys in the houses it eats.

THE END

THE FOUR-HEADED PIE THROWER

The four-headed pie thrower throws pies. It eats ice cream. It drinks melted ice cream. It throws pies at other monsters. Its favorite word is the end.

THE END

Note the common thread throughout all three stories—eating! As Paley (1990) suggests, in a story a child says, "This is how I interpret and translate right now something that is on my mind." Obviously, eating was on this child's mind. She was, through story, making sense for herself of our earlier conversation.

Students should be encouraged to use stories to "make sense," to enhance their learning. Wells (1986) writes:

> Constructing stories in the mind—or storying, as it has been called—is one of the most fundamental means of making meaning; as such, it is an activity that pervades all aspects of learning. When storying becomes overt and is given expression in words, the resulting stories are one of the most effective ways of making one's own interpretation of events and ideas available to others. Through the exchange of stories, therefore, teachers and students can share their understandings of a topic and bring their mental models of the world into closer alignment. In this sense, stories and storying are relevant in all areas of the curriculum. (p. 194)

Schoafsma (1989) concurs:

> We who teach often dismiss stories as a primitive form, a form for children, something students need to move "beyond" for the learning they will have to do in schools. However, stories, grounded as they are in students' lives and concerns, are one important means students have for making sense of their worlds, an important tool for learning. (p. 89)

Note the following story written by an eight-year-old, in which she "makes sense" of one aspect of natural life:

HOW THE OCEAN GOT ITS FOAM

Once a cloud fell in the ocean.
When the cloud put itself back together,
he couldn't get all itself
so some was left.
So that's how
the ocean got its foam.

As students share their concerns, desires, fears, accomplishments, and dreams through their stories, they become members of what Bruner calls a "culture creating community" (p. 132). According to Bruner, "It is not just that the child must make his knowledge his own, but that he must make it his own in a community of those who share his sense of belonging to a culture" (p. 120).

Much schooling today is what James Paul Gee (1986) refers to as essay-text literacy: "Essay-text literacy... is connected with the forms of consciousness and the interests of the powerful in our society" (p. 742). Essay-text literacy is efficient, neatly packaged knowledge. It allows little room for knowledge gained from personal experience. For true learning, narrative knowledge is essential. Narrative knowledge is experiential and cultural knowing. It is the best means available for students to organize their experiences and make meaning for themselves.

Students are not the only ones who should tell stories in the classroom. Obviously, both you and your students will become the teacher-tellers when storytelling is used as a teaching strategy. What grade level or what subject matter you teach really matters little. Elements of storytelling can be used at all levels and in all subjects. A few examples follow; you will recognize many of these as methods you already employ. Storytelling can be used:

- to introduce a unit (explaining to students how you reacted to the assassination of John F. Kennedy could be an effective way to introduce a high school history unit, for example).
- to help explain a concept (a story about a young child's reaction to the first day of school could be used to clarify child development concepts in a family relations class).
- to set the stage for a science experiment (a story about how scientists first decided to do the experiment would be good here).

The possibilities are endless. I remember a high school teacher who, prior to our dissecting a frog, told our sophomore biology class the story of the wide-mouthed frog. (This is a story usually told to younger children. It involves a wide-mouthed frog who travels through the woods asking forest creatures what they feed their babies. The frog finally meets a snake, who replies "wide-mouth frogs.") He explained to us that, although we were using frogs for scientific purposes, we should always remember that frogs are special creatures!

Thus, storytelling can be used across the curriculum and is a powerful teaching tool for several reasons.

Storytelling allows the teacher to provide instruction indirectly

It is easy to embed teaching lessons, information, and mental processes in story form. It is one thing to instruct students in character-building by telling them that "virtue wins over evil" and quite another to relate the story of "Cinderella." The story is far richer psychologically in providing a concrete and understandable lesson on the rewards of virtue. The complex, often multilayered, tapestries of stories provide students with much food for thought.

Storyteller Syd Lieberman suggests that it is the *story* in *history* that provides the nail on which to hang facts. Students remember historical facts when they are tied to a story. Livo and Rietz (1986) report that a high school in Boulder, Colorado, experimented with a study of presentation of historical material. Storytellers present material in dramatic context to the students, and group discussion follows. Students are encouraged to read further. In contrast, another group of students is involved in traditional research/report techniques. The study at this stage indicates that the material presented by the storytellers has much more interest and personal impact than that gained via the traditional method.

Storytelling prompts questions and conversations

Storytelling is both a way to prompt questions and conversation. For teachers, questions are the single most influential teaching practice because questions determine which mental processes students engage in, which points of a topic students can explore, and which modes of thought students learn (Cooper, 1995). In addition, research suggests that conversation—students discussing, arguing, orally creating ideas—enhances learning (Cooper, 1995).

As Richard Lewis (1979) suggests:

> One of the ways I look at education is that it is an attempt to elicit response—that to educate means, in effect, to allow the individual to reverberate enough experiences and ideas within himself that he needs to respond. The need to respond is the beginning of framing and forming knowledge so that it becomes understandable for one's self. So going back to the story, it seems to me the story is a kind of melodic line that has a built-in need for response. So when the story brings out questions, it has started a melody which has to be continued by the hearer in some way, either through the response of a question or some other reflection of what the story may have meant for him. (p. 69)

Learning becomes fun when stories are used

When questioned about their favorite teacher, many people relate effective storytelling as the quality they remember most, not the ability to organize material or profound knowledge of the subject. One high school student put it this way: "When Mrs. Nicholson told us stories about why she wanted to become a science teacher—what things fascinated her and why—we began to love science, too. I don't know why, exactly. But, somehow, I wanted to discover things, too, to see them as she saw them. Learning became a fun challenge."

In her investigation of the storytellng activity of teachers, Holladay (1987) concludes that teachers who use story are more effective than those who do not. Positive relationships between students and teacher are enhanced through storytelling. In addition, students are better able to relate the content of the course to their personal lives when the teacher uses stories to explain course content.

Let me give you some specific examples. Suppose you are teaching history. Regardless of the grade level you teach, you might use oral histories as a way to help students understand how history "works" in their own lives. I have observed teachers who ask students to collect oral histories of their family members, particularly grandparents and great-grandparents. After collecting these oral histories, students create and tell their own genealogies, beginning with their great-great grandparents and following through to their parents.

> I am the great-great grandson of an itinerant farmer—a man who loved the feel of dirt in his hands and the sun on his face—and a woman who kept the farm's books and household and raised five children. I am the great-grandson of a man who loved learning and taught in a one-room schoolhouse and a woman who was the first librarian in a small Kansas town. I am the son of…

The storyteller presents some brief information about each ancestor. The students could even include information about brothers, sisters, cousins, and so on.

Another successful teaching tool is to have students research famous historical characters and present genealogies for them. The popularity of the 1990 documentary *The Civil War,* presented on public television, should indicate to us all how history can be brought to life through personal stories.

If you are a math teacher, you might have students make up and tell one another story problems. Ask them to share a personal story in which a math error caused them problems. If you teach science, create a unit on "Scientific Myths" or "How Physics Came to Be." If using the scientific myths suggestion, you might tell stories from Rudyard Kipling's *Just So Stories* about how certain animals got their major characteristics, then move to more recent myths of science that have been dispelled.

In sum, through research and through personal experience we learn more every day about the central role that storytelling plays in empowering teacher and students to synthesize and verbalize personal experiences, communicate feelings, and construct meaning—processes vital to effective learning.

Conclusion

I have always loved I. B. Singer's reminder in *Naftali the Storyteller and His Horse, Sus:**

---

* Excerpt from *Naftali the Storyteller and His Horse, Sus* by Isaac Bashevis Singer, translated by Joseph Singer. Copyright © 1973, 1976 by Isaac Bashevis Singer. Reprinted by permission of Farrar, Straus & Giroux, Inc.

When a day passes it is no longer there.
What remains of it? Nothing more than a story.
If stories weren't told or books weren't written, man would live like beasts—
    only for the day.
Today, we live, but tomorrow today will be a story.
The whole world, all human life, is one long story.

This same idea is expressed at the end of the Chinese folktale "White Wave":

When the old man died, the shell was lost.
In time, the shrine, too, disappeared. All that remained was the story.
But that is how it is with all of us.
When we die, all that remains is the story.

Often, as I struggle to think of stories to use in my own teaching, I remember this and wonder, "What happened in my experience (what I've done or read) that I can use to help my students make sense of this content?" Without fail, I find a story that works! I also say this to children when I want them to tell a story. I say it, and then I ask, "So, what's a story you can tell about today, before it slips away?"

SUGGESTED READINGS

Hardyment, Christina. 1989. *Heidi's Alp: One Family's Search for Storybook Europe*. New York: Atlantic Monthly Press.

This is the story of the journey the author and her four daughters took across Europe. They set out to trace the roots of stories that have captured the imaginations of generations of children.

Paley, Vivian. 1990. *The Boy Who Would Be a Helicopter*. Cambridge, MA: Harvard University Press.

This book is the diary of a year in the evolving drama of a preschool classroom and the role story plays.

Pellowski, Ann. 1990. *The World of Storytelling*. New York: H. W. Wilson.

An excellent text for those interested in the history of storytelling. The first seven chapters are devoted to the history of storytelling in numerous cultures.

Stotter, Ruth. 1995. *About Story*. Stinson Beach, CA: Stotter Press.

Written by the director of the interdisciplinary storytelling program at Dominican College, this text offers rich essays about the functions and traditions of storytelling.

Meet the storyteller...
Caitlin Collins

Photo by Dawn Murray

*Caitlin is a lively, charming seven-year-old.
It was easy to interview Rives' daughter Caitlin
because she and I like each other very much
and also, Caitlin is a talker!*

Q: What are some of your favorite stories?

A: Oh, that's a very hard question. I like so
many. I like true stories, but I also like fantasy.
I really like my dad's stories about when he was
young, especially the ones about when he got
into trouble. His father was very strict about manners, and my dad's manners weren't always the best.

Q: What kind of stories do you like to tell?

A: I like to tell stories I've read in a book.

Q: Why?

A: Because I can picture everything in my mind and tell it, but I don't tell it
with the same words the author did. I can tell a story after hearing it only
once. My teacher read us a story recently called "How Snoeshoe Hair Saved
the Sun." I could picture the story in my mind, and then I told it.

Q: Why did you like that story?

A: It was kind of silly, and I like silly stories. But most of all, I liked it because
it reminded me of something I am trying to work on my own life—not brag-
ging. I'm really working on that and so the story reminded me not to brag.

  Another thing I should tell you is that when I hear a story I really like, I
type it into my computer. Sometimes I even leave a space to draw a picture.
Anyway, then when I'm bored, I go to the computer and open my file and
read my favorite stories over again. So, I have a book of my own of my
favorite stories. I like that.

Q: So, a good story is something you can go back to?

A: Yes. There are some stories you just never grow tired of.

Q: Would you rather have someone read you a story or tell you a story?

A: Well, that sort of depends on whether the person is a good storyteller.
My teacher mostly reads stories to us, but she wants to become a better storyteller. Now she's trying to learn to tell stories. So not long ago, she told us
a story about staying with her mother and weeding in the garden, and acci-
dentally stepping on a hill of fire ants. Luckily, there was a hose nearby so
she could spray the ants off of herself, but still they stung. Those bites hurt

really, really, really bad—for a whole week. After she told us the story, we all wrote it down together. That helps her learn to tell a good story, and it helps us learn to be good writers. Now we're working on a story she told us about chipmunks that she watched when she was at her mother's house.

Q: Is your teacher getting to be a better storyteller?

A: Oh, yes.

Q: Why do you think that is?

A: Well, she's getting better at telling stories by telling more stories.

Q: Do you like to tell stories?

A: Oh, very much. I wrote a story called "Kirsty and the Leprechaun," which I gave my mother for St. Patrick's Day. It's nice to give stories as gifts. I also wrote another story, "Jenny and the Dog."

Q: Did you make that one up or did you hear it somewhere?

A: I got inspired by one of the Boxcar Children books. I really like those books because the children never complain and I love the adventure and mystery in the books. Sometimes, and this happens with books other than the Boxcar Children books, when my mother says, "OK, Caitlin, it's time to turn out the lights and go to sleep," I'm tempted to sneak the light on after she leaves my room and finish the part I'm on. Of course, I never do, but I am tempted!

Q: Do you ever tell your brother Ethan stories?

A: Yes; you know he can't read. But sometimes he tells the story in a book to me. He makes it up from the pictures. I used to do that too, and I think that it's a good thing. It encourages Ethan to look at books and stories. So, I'm supportive. I never say, "That's not what it says," because that would make him not like books and stories.

Maybe I should tell you a story. You know I said I like stories that are true and I like fantasy too? Well, this is a story that my dad and I made up together and you'll see that some is true and some is fantasy. It's about a Saturday morning when my mom was at aerobics class, so my dad was in charge. It's pretty wild when my dad is in charge, if you know what I mean. So here's the story.

(Caitlin told me a story about her father's attempts to change Ethan's diapers as Caitlin blew bubbles out the window. Ethan ends up in a bubble and the chase is on. Through a series of events, they all end up at Baskin Robbins, where Ethan has bubble gum ice cream, blows a bubble and starts to float away again, but is saved by Caitlin. The story lasted ten minutes, complete with movement and voice changes. Caitlin filled my family room as she animated the story.)

It's fun to tell that story again and again. You know, I don't know if this happens to others, but it does to me. When I first start telling a story, like I did for you just now, I feel nervous. But once you get started, you don't feel nervous anymore. You just want to tell the story.

Meet the storyteller...

Jamie Hoel

Jamie is 12 years old. In addition to telling stories (she and her mother often do story-telling performances together), her hobbies are ice skating, playing the violin, reading, and biking, and she loves to travel.

Photo by Dawn Murray

Q: Why do you like stories?

A: Well, if there were no stories, there would be nothing to say or do because everything you say is a story.

Q: Why do you like writing stories?

A: Mostly because I like stories, and if you couldn't write stories, you couldn't write anything.

Q: Where do you get your stories?

A: From my imagination. Sometimes I write about personal experiences.

Q: After you write a story, what do you do with it?

A: Usually, I type it on my computer. All of my stories are there so I can continue to work on them.

Q: When you tell a story, what kind of story do you like to tell?

A: I like telling spooky stories because people love them. You also have fun telling them. You can imitate the monster or speak like the ghost.

Q: What's the difference between reading *The Wizard of Oz* and seeing the movie?

A: Well, the movie you get to see with your eyes. When you read a book, you have to make up the pictures in your mind. *You* have to show the pictures to *you*, because there's no TV or movie screen.

Q: Which is better?

A: I like reading because then you can "see" it over and over and make up new pictures every time. If you watch the movie, you see the same pictures over and over, and that gets boring.

Q: If you want to be a good storyteller, what should you do?

A: Tell stories a lot. Tell stories you think are good stories. If you really want to be a good storyteller, you should use different voices when you need to. For example, if a person in the story is mean, you should use a mean voice and make a mean face—stuff like that.

CHAPTER 2
· ·
This Is Why I Tell It:
The Value of Telling Stories

A Zuni once asked an anthropologist, who was carefully writing down a story,
"When I tell these stories, do you see it, or do you just write it down?"

Dennis Tedlock

BECAUSE I am interested in how storytelling empowers teachers and learners alike in the learning process, I'll focus on twelve reasons storytelling is valuable. Some of these reasons are a result of listening to stories; some are the result of telling them.

Enhances imagination and visualization

Storyteller Jay O'Callahan defines storytelling as the "theater of the mind." The storyteller provides the skeleton; the listener adds the "flesh" of scenery, character, and so on. As such, the listener has to visualize what the character and setting look like. Consider the following opening to the story of *Wilfrid Gordon McDonald Partridge* by Mem Fox (1985):

> There once was a small boy called Wilfrid Gordon McDonald Partridge and what's more he wasn't very old either.

The listener must imagine how Gordon looks, how old he is, his hair color, color of his eyes, his height. In addition, the listener has to imagine the characters Gordon knows: Mrs. Jordan who played the organ, Mr. Hosking who told scary stories, Mr. Tippit who was crazy about cricket, Mrs. Mitchell who walked with a wooden stick, Mr. Drysdale who had a voice like a giant, and Miss Nancy Alison Delacourt Cooper to whom Wilfrid told all his secrets.

The ability to visualize, to create images in the mind, is at the very heart of storytelling, not just for the listener, but also for the teller. To create the visualization and images in the listener's mind, the storyteller must have a clear visual image in her own mind. For example, if the storyteller is trying to create a visual image of Wilfrid Gordon, she will need to recall all the little boys she's known, create a composite, and see that image in her mind's eye before she can create the image for her audience. The same is true for any character and for any audience. I recently told this same story for a group of adults at a storytelling workshop. Afterward, a man of about 50 came up and said, "That story touched me more than you can imagine. My mother suffers from Alzheimer's disease, and Miss Nancy reminded me of her."

Develops appreciation of the beauty and rhythm of language

My students are constantly amazed at how quickly children "chime in" when a story has a refrain. As children chant a refrain—"King Bidgood's in the bathtub and he won't get out, oh, who knows what to do? Who knows what to do?" or, "Tikki Tikki Tembo-no sa rembo chari-beri richi-pip peri pembo," or "It's Heckedy Peg. She's lost her leg. They let her in," or "I do not like them, Sam-I-am. I do not like green eggs and ham"—with the storyteller, they begin to understand the beauty of their own language as well as its power to create an image and an emotion.

Think about the range of language students encounter in a story—unfamiliar words, archaic expressions, puns, words, and phrases used in unique ways. While at a storytelling festival recently I heard again Rudyard Kipling's "The Elephant's Child" and again was enthralled with the language. Who can fail to appreciate descriptions such as "the nose no bigger than a bulgy boot," "satiable curiosity," the "banks of the great grey-green greasy Limpopo River, all set about the fever trees..." Aidan Chalmers (1973) suggests the full range of language usage that storytelling makes possible:

> As children listen to stories, verse, prose of all kinds, they unconsciously become familiar with the rhythms and structure, the cadences and conventions of the various forms of written language. They are learning how print "sounds," how to "hear" it in their inner ear. Only through listening to words in print being spoken does anyone discover their colour, their life, their movement and drama. (p. 181)

As students get older, this "full range of language" can continue to be enhanced. During one of my children's literature classes, a young college football player decided he wanted to tell the story "The Little Engine That Could." When I asked him why, he told me this story:

> I come from a very small high school in a remote part of Nebraska. We never won many football games. Our team was getting pretty discouraged. We all wanted to quit. The coach came in one day before a game and told us the story "The Little Engine That Could." We played pretty good that day! Before every game after that, we ran onto the field yelling in unison, "I think I can! I think I can!" Isn't that the greatest story?! It changed my life! Ever since then, those words "I think I can" have helped me through a lot!

Note that this student learned no new words. But he did learn the power of language!

Increases vocabulary

Students may not know the meaning of all words they hear, but they will understand them from the context. Storyteller Betty Weeks provides the following example. In her version of "The Three Bears," she uses the phrase "arrested by a constable and put in a house of correction." She reports having the following conversation:

Child:	Mrs. Weeks, what's a constable?
Mrs. Weeks:	What do you think?
Child:	A policeman. What's that "house of correction?"
Mrs. Weeks:	What do you think?
Child:	A jail.

Refines speaking skills

In its document, *Essential Speaking and Listening Skills for Elementary School Students,* the Speech Communication Association (1993) lists seventeen oral communication competencies. Similarly, the document *Speaking and Listening Competencies for High School Graduates* (1993) lists fifteen oral communication competencies. Among these thirty-two competencies to be developed for grades K–12 are:

- Speak clearly and expressively through appropriate articulation, pronunciation, volume, rate, and intonation.
- Organize messages so others can understand them.
- Use and understand spoken language appropriate to the context (e.g., topic, purpose, audience).
- Use nonverbal cues that emphasize meaning.
- Clarify and support ideas with necessary details.
- Recognize when another does not understand the message.

The most valuable learning occurs when a real purpose is involved. Storytelling can help students refine their speaking skills because a real purpose—telling a story—is involved. For example, when telling a story, students should use gestures and body movement, organize the story in a sequence easily understandable to the listeners, speak clearly—all for the purpose of making the story enjoyable for the listener. As Livo and Rietz (1986) indicate, variables such as intonation, pause, gesture, and body language are to the storyteller what hammer and nails are to the carpenter (p. 345). When children and adolescents retell a story they've heard, they practice their speaking skills. Teachers should encourage retellings. Betty Weeks, a kindergarten teacher, provides one technique to promote retelling:

> I always tell stories at the end of the day because I want children to leave school with the story in their heads. Often they retell the story to their parents on the way home or to their brothers and sisters. So it really does enhance oral language.

Improves listening skills

The Speech Communication Association suggests the following listening competencies to be developed, which storytelling can enhance:

- Listen effectively to spoken messages (hear the speaker, understand meaning, follow sequence of ideas, draw inferences).
- Recognize and interpret nonverbal cues others give.
- Provide effective and appropriate feedback.
- Critically evaluate a spoken message.

When a child listens to a story, she not only hears the words but also understands meanings and draws inferences and interprets the storyteller's nonverbal messages. While she listens, she provides feedback—a smile, chiming in on a refrain, and so on. She also can be encouraged to evaluate critically the story she hears. Does it make sense in terms of her life experiences? Did she like the story? Why or why not?

Allows students to interact with adults on a personal level

The power of the relationship that can be created is often surprising to education students. When they venture into classrooms to tell stories, they are, at first, somewhat uncomfortable with the closeness that occurs. Young children tend to crowd close to the storyteller, often wanting to sit on her lap or touch her. They shout, "Tell us another! Tell us another!" or, "Come back tomorrow!" Often they ask questions about the storyteller's life: "Are you married? Where do you live? How old are you?"

This relationship building can occur when the teacher tells a story about himself. It may be the first inkling students have that this teacher is a real person, one who grocery shops, goes to the movies, has fears and frustrations. This sort of knowledge is what builds a relationship. I sit in the classroom of teacher-teller Betty Weeks. I watch the kindergarten children sitting at her feet (almost on them!). Their eyes tell it all. They cannot wait for her to begin. This is a teacher they will remember always. This story time is special. No matter what else has happened during the day, they leave with a story.

Enhances writing skills

Essentials of English (National Council of Teachers of English, 1982) is a document that states as its purpose: "to identify the ways in which the study of English contributes to the knowledge, understanding, and skills of those who will make up the society of the future."

In the section focusing on writing skills, the following objectives are outlined:

- Learn to write clearly and honestly.
- Recognize that writing is a way to learn and develop personally, as well as a way to communicate with others.
- Learn ways to generate ideas for writing, to select and arrange them, to find appropriate modes for expressing them, and to evaluate and revise what they have written.
- Learn to adapt expression to various audiences.

Storytelling can help enhance writing skills. By hearing and telling stories, students learn to write their own stories, and by doing so they master the objectives above. Let me give you an example of how this can work. Several years ago I was teaching a course entitled, "Presentational Forms of Children's Literature." One group of students was interested in writing stories to perform. They contacted a junior high school and got permission to interview eighth-graders. They asked the eighth-graders to tell them about their hobbies, their concerns, their fears, things they like to do, and their most embarrassing moments. In essence, they asked the eighth-graders, "Tell us your story of what it's like to be an eighth-grader." My students then wrote stories utilizing the information they gathered, and then they performed them for the eighth-graders. The title of the performance was, "A Day in the Life of an Eighth-Grader." After the performance, my students discussed with the eighth-graders how well they had captured the essence of an eighth-grader's day. This experience gave my students a chance to utilize storytelling to enhance their writing skills.

Develops reading skills and sparks an interest in reading

In my storytelling classes I am amazed at how much literature students read to find "just the right story" to tell. As they read, they search for the story's meaning and analyze and evaluate the literature. In addition, they find pleasure in reading. Thus, storytelling enhances reading skills.

At the conclusion of the performances in schools, I like to share a secret with the children. "Would you like to know where I get my stories?" I ask in my best conspiratorial voice. "It's a secret, but I'll tell you if you promise not to blab it around." By now, I am speaking in a whisper; the children are leaning forward to hear. "I get my stories" (eyes move left and right to make sure nobody is spying on us) "...I get my stories from..." (pause; I look them in the eyes and mouth the next words without making a sound "...the library. Shhh! Don't tell anybody! It can be our secret. Just remember: Everything I told today—and a whole lot more—can be found right here in your school l-i-b-r-a-r-y."

I have learned it is a good idea to warn librarians and media specialists before I do this. They report stampedes: Where are the Norse legends? Can you help me find the 398 section? Do we have *Jumanji*? Where can I find the stories by Edgar Allan Poe? Do we have African folktales? After a storytelling performance, the library becomes a very busy place.

Teachers for junior high and high school students report similar experiences. For example, after being told a story from *The Time-Ago Tales of Jahdu*, several members of a junior level English class rushed to the library to get other books by Virginia Hamilton. One junior high English teacher recently read to her eighth graders the Newbery Award-winning book *The True Confessions of Charlotte Doyle*. After a lively discussion of what growing up female means and what growing up male means in our society, students asked to read more books in which those issues are considered.

Enhances critical and creative thinking skills

Stories that have riddles or problems to solve are particularly helpful in enhancing creative/critical thinking skills. Betty Weeks likes to illustrate this idea with her telling of the Welsh tale, "Morgan and His Pot of Brains." Poor Morgan, you see, was just not very bright. As the villagers would say, "Intelligence was not a burden he had been asked to bear." More than anything, he wanted the pot of brains from the little man so he would know how to make his way in the world. In this rather grisly story, Morgan must do the bidding of the little man who stands grinning over the simmering pot of brains. Each time Morgan returns with the heart of the thing he loves most dearly in all the world, the little man confronts him with a riddle: "What shines and is yellow but is not gold?" Morgan doesn't know. "What is old, old, old, yet is new every month?" Morgan doesn't know. "What runs all day without moving?" Morgan hasn't a clue.

The riddles are never answered in the story. When it is finished, the children's hands shoot up. It has been a story rich with suspense and strong feeling, but often the children are still curious about the riddles. While children are feeling, they are also thinking. Perhaps like Morgan, they long to have enough sense to make their way in the world. Hours later a child may shout, "The moon, Mrs. Weeks. It's the moon."

A powerful story I often tell to high school and college students is "Many Moons," by James Thurber. I like to tell this story because lively discussions ensue about the relationships among the characters, the real nature of each character, who fools whom, and so forth. Thus, students are asked to think critically. In addition, I encourage them to think creatively in a follow-up activity. I ask students to create stories that are of the "what's it made of" or "how did the stars get into the sky" variety.

Nourishes students' intuitive side

Storytelling involves much more than regurgitating or creating content. It involves a feeling: How does the storyteller feel about the characters? The story's theme? His audience? Not often can we, as teachers, involve our students' whole brains, their thinking and feeling, at the same time. In storytelling we can. For example, when I tell the story "The Gift of the Magi," I am not just telling a story about a wife who sells her hair to buy a watch chain for her husband, who has sold his watch to buy combs for her long, beautiful hair. That's not a great story. The great story occurs when I feel the wife's great love that enables her to make the sacrifice (I, too, have always coveted long, beautiful hair, so I can relate to the sacrifice in a personal way) and the feeling she has when she discovers her husband's love is great enough that he has sold his most valued possession to buy her a gift. When I keep these feelings close to my heart as I tell, I am a better storyteller.

In addition, much of our schooling focuses on our logical side. Our feelings are often negated when they are expressed. But storytelling says, "Hey, it's okay to feel. Feelings are valid. Feelings are what make us human; they are a part of what we are." Storytelling allows us to express our feelings. We can laugh or cry.

Helps students see literature as a mirror of human experience

Storytelling reflects human motives, frailties, values, and conflicts. In his book *The Uses of Enchantment: The Meaning and Importance of Fairytales,* Bruno Bettelheim (1975) suggests that folktales are recipes for examining the human condition. He argues that fairytales enable children to learn about human progress and about possible solutions to human problems. Children learn that struggling against difficulties is unavoidable, but if they confront the unexpected or unjust hardships directly, they can emerge victorious. As Maguire (1985) suggests:

> Storytelling gives children more scope for working out their dreamlike perceptions of life, for symbolically confronting its myriad opportunities and difficulties. It equips them with tools—images and words—that they can use to test their intuition and powers of judgement; and it safely and gently introduces topics that can later be discussed openly outside of the privileged world of storytelling. (p. 20)

Every story is told to say something about what life means. Stories help us make sense of our experiences and understand the experiences of others. How wonderful it is when we connect through story, when we can say, "That reminds me of the time I…" or, "I've had that same feeling…"

Helps students understand their own and others' cultural heritage

One of the best ways to understand our own culture is by hearing stories. I give the students in my children's literature class an assignment that helps them understand this. I explain to them that folklore is the lore of the folk, so all people have folklore. I then ask them to divide into small groups and tell one another the folklore of their university. One story is about the ghost in University Hall. Another story explains why the sorority houses are on one end of campus and the fraternity houses on the other. I then ask them to explain why those stories got started and passed down, what they say about what it means to be a Northwestern University student. I also ask them to think about the lore of their family and how the stories they are told about various members of their family help to give them their identity. For example, what do the stories of my Grandfather Cooper tell me about who I am, about what it means to be a part of the Cooper clan?

Storytelling is also a way of helping students understand a culture different from their own. As Ann Nolan Clark (1969) writes:

> Children need to know of other nationalities and races so that, inheriting an adult world, they find a free and joyous interchange of acceptance and respect among all peoples…. There is a need for awareness that each group of people has its own special traditions and customs. There is a need for acceptance of these differences. There is tragic need for loving communion between children and children, children and adults, adults and adults— between group and group. (p. 89)

As storyteller Syd Lieberman suggests, "If you want to study another culture, what better way than to hear it through stories." I was a visitor to Ireland several years ago. Beforehand, I decided to see if I really could understand a culture by reading its stories, so I read Irish folktales, lots of Irish folktales. The more I read, the more I began to understand. When I got to Ireland, I felt a sense of "at homeness."

When I was a visiting scholar at the Chinese University of Hong Kong, I used storytelling as the major teaching strategy in my oral communication classroom. As a result of my using personal experience and folktales to teach intercultural communication, students not only learned communication principles but also applied these principles to different cultures. That is, the stories helped students understand communication in cultures different from their own. (Cooper, 1994)

Conclusion

In the book *The Talking Bird and the Story Pouch*, Amy Lawson (1987) tells the story of a reluctant storyteller, a young man whose father handed down the Story Pouch and the Talking Bird, the necessities of a storyteller. The boy does not really wish to be a storyteller, and so he does not gather stories, nor does he tell them. His mother warns him that unless he does so, he will lose the Talking Bird, the charm that helps him find stories to put in his story pouch. Not until the storyteller sets off on a journey and tells his stories to those he meets does he begin to see the value in the occupation handed down to him by his father. In this chapter I've outlined many of those values. Like the young man, you'll recognize those values as you tell your own stories and hear the stories of others.

SUGGESTED READINGS

Brett, Doris. 1988. *Annie's Stories.* New York: Workman.

> *Based on her experience with her own daughter, the author provides stories to help children cope with real-life situations and explains how parents can adapt the stories to their individual circumstance.*

Coles, Robert. 1980. "Children's stories: The link to a past." *Children's Literature* 8: 141–146.

> *Cole writes about children's "natural" development of an interest in story and its role in their lives.*

Wallace-Brodeur, R. 1989. *Stories from the Big Chair.* New York: Macmillan.

> *This book contains seven stories, one for each day of the week. They are told by a little girl named Molly, who is tired of her little sister, Susan. The stories she tells help her better understand herself and Susan.*

National Storytelling Association. 1996. *National Storytelling Directory.* Jonesborough, TN: National Storytelling Press.

> *This directory lists storytellers, organizations, events, periodicals, educational opportunities, broadcast programming, and production companies dealing with storytelling. It also includes several articles. A super resource!*

Meet the storyteller...

Anne Shimojima

Photo by Luanna B. Bleveans

Anne Shimojima is a full-time school library media specialist at the Braeside School in Highland Park, Illinois. A freelance storyteller who specializes in folktales from around the world, she is also a member of the board of directors of the Wild Onion Storytelling Celebration.

Q: So, Anne, you're a full-time librarian?

A: Well, I'm actually called school library media specialist now.

Q: School library media specialist. At Braeside School in Highland Park. How long have you been doing that?

A: For 21 years. Before that I taught school in Chicago on the south side for one year.

Q: Great. Can you tell us how storytelling is a part of your Instructional Media Center?

A: I use storytelling to share the gift of story, to lead children to books, and to support and extend the curriculum. And there are a lot of ways you can bring storytelling in. I bring it in whenever I can because I love to do it so much and because the kids love it so much. For instance, in kindergarten and first grade, we do it with creative drama where I tell a story and the kids act it out. In second grade, they do a very big unit on folktales and fairytales. And because we're flexibly scheduled we can schedule according to need. So during the six or eight weeks of a particular unit, the classes come in every day for a combination of reading and telling. We might tell folktales from all different continents when we're working on continents in geography. And I tell stories.

A culminating activity is that we create a picture book where I tell a story and then we divide it into scenes. Each child gets a scene and then has to rewrite just that part of the story, so it's not the burden of rewriting the *whole* story. I type it on paper and they illustrate it and then every child gets a copy of the entire picture book.

What's amazing to me is that they'll be able to tell me the story back. I'll do long stories because we have to get twenty-four, or however many kids there are, scenes in there. So I'm doing things like "Wiley and the Hairy Man," which is a wonderful story. And I'll tell that story once and say, "Okay, what's the first thing you remember?" And by golly, they know the whole story.

Q: What grade?

A: Second.

Q: Wow!

A: And I mean, they've heard stories since kindergarten. And they've heard a lot of stories. But it still amazes me that they can hear a story of that complexity and give it right back to me. In third grade, we do a "Jack Tale" unit—I tell all my Jack Tales (like Jack in the Beanstalk—there are lots of stories about Jack) then. And again, we draw pictures—a favorite part, remembered images.

We retell stories. A lot of times, I'll put the kids in a circle and have them retell a story round robin.

Another culminating activity is to do a video. It's just like the picture book, but instead of putting it into book form, the kids draw big 12-by-18-inch pictures and then I videotape the pictures while they read their parts. In fifth grade, we do a very big Native American unit and each child has to learn and tell a Native American legend. So at that point, I'm taking them in small groups and helping them learn how to tell stories. In fourth and fifth grade, I meet with the kids over a period of four to five weeks and I tell stories and they rewrite them, so it becomes a writing activity. I think it's very good for recall and sequencing and vocabulary. We urge them to add detail to the story, and we talk about what can be changed and what can't be changed. They can't change the plot or the ending, only the details, so they're very creative in how they do that.

Q: Tell me about working to help your fifth-graders be storytellers. How do you do that?

A: The first thing I do is tell a very short story. They've heard stories all through their years. But I say, "This time, when you listen to me tell a story, I want you to pay attention to how I'm doing it, okay? Watch what I'm doing with my hands and my voice and my eyes." And then afterwards, I'll say, "Now, what did you notice?" "Well, you looked at all of us right in the eye." "You didn't look at one person. You looked at everybody." Or, "Your voice went up and down." Or, "You used your hands," or whatever. And we talk about the components of storytelling. They all choose a story to learn.

Q: Is that process important? The process of choosing a story?

A: Oh, absolutely, because I think you're most successful with a story that you personally connect with and like a lot. I mean, that's half of it right there. And I think they have ownership and a sense of power that they can choose the story. We have a very large collection of Native American legends that they choose from.

Q: So one of the other things you're teaching is research. They're going through collections finding a story...

A: Right. And what makes a good story.

Q: Do they have to read several stories before they find one that works?

A: Absolutely. Yes. And then we do a story map, which is a chart that divides the story into protagonist, antagonist, initial action, problems...

makes them constantly look at the structure of their story as an aid to learning. We say, "You're not memorizing this story. And be conscious of why you chose this story. What did you like about it?" Then, the next time we get together, they get up and tell their stories. We all give positive comments as well as ideas to help them make this a better story. We continue to meet and every time we meet, they're retelling their stories and you can see they're getting more and more polished, they know it better and better. At the end, they tell the story in class. They create, through the research in the library, a museum in their room. We've divided it up into regions—here's the Northwest region, the Plains region, the Southwest. They've created basically a museum exhibit of their region. They've created artifacts and charts and pictures and as part of it, they tell the story.

Q: Oh, that's great.

A: It's a very involved, long unit.

Q: Do they dread the storytelling?

A: Oh no! I think they might be a little nervous at the beginning because they haven't done this before, but I think they enjoy it. They look on story-telling as a really enjoyable thing. I think they like being storytellers.

Q: Is there understanding that comes from learning the stories of another culture?

A: I think it gives you a different facet of the culture. And it's a very important facet—one that often is missed when people are concerned only with information. I think if you're going to do any kind of cultural setting, you bring in the stories of the people to better understand the culture.

Q: Can we shift gears for a second? You know that I came to storytelling from the world of theater. You came from a different place. Is that right?

A: Yes, yes. I came from the library, which is really different from theater, because theater focuses on performance, and we don't come to storytelling from performance at all. We think of it in terms of bringing literature to children and enticing them to read books with the sounds of the words. When I got into this, I wasn't thinking at all about being a performance artist or anything like that. And at the school, I'm more concerned with the educational end of it.

Q: Can you describe your style?

A: I have a very straightforward, fairly quiet style. I'm not adding the flash; the substance has to come from the stories. I don't have a musical instrument with me. I'm not a stand-up comic. I'm not an actor. I'm drawn to stories that are strong in plot, that have meaning.

Q: Have you learned not to apologize for your style?

A: It gets intimidating when you see people perform who are very funny or who are very theatrical. But I have been told that my style allows the story to come through really clearly.

Q: Do you want to comment at all about being an Asian American storyteller?

A: I'm Japanese American and my parents did not lay a whole lot on me verbally. When I became a storyteller, to my great surprise, I ran up against this Japanese thing that we shouldn't stand out in the crowd. Because Japanese psychology is group psychology. Everybody blends into the group. And all of a sudden I was finding myself up in front of the room with a large group of people all looking at me. And this Japanese-ness just came out in me that I didn't know existed and I had to get over it. And in getting over it, I discovered that I liked being a storyteller and people's attention being on me because it was happening in a very positive way. So I look at storytelling as helping me grow past my cultural limitations. But I think part of growing old and maturing is that you have to grow beyond where you came from. There aren't very many Asian storytellers so I get called on more and more to do the Asian stories. When I started storytelling, I was not looking for Asian stories, I was just looking for a good story. It's hard enough to find a story. I mean you can read thirty or forty stories until you find one you want to spend the time to learn to tell. But as I've been asked to tell Asian stories, I've had to spend some time looking for them. I like it. It's made me disciplined.

Q: In this era of "back to basics," "test scores," and "high technology," why do you think storytelling is so important?

A: Storytelling does what all good art does. It lifts us to the best of what being human is. It brings us all together. Storytelling connects us with the part of ourselves that responds to truth and beauty. I love my work, but storytelling is my bliss.

CHAPTER 3

• •

We All Have Stories:
Discovering Personal Narratives

> *"The lines in a face tell a story;*
> *the lines in a face sing a song.*
> *The lines are a keepsake of moments gone by,*
> *choices we've made, right or wrong.*
> *And we earn our lines from our stories:*
> *We earn our lines from our songs.*
> *Trace the pattern and the story unwinds,*
> *Who we are is in the lines left behind."*
>
> *Singer/Songwriter Julie Shannon*

WITHIN THE national resurgence of storytelling, there is one distinctive genre that seems to be growing particularly rapidly—family stories. Also known as personal narratives, these tales about the people and places we have known are taking on new meaning and significance. Some of our nation's most prominent tellers are choosing to share family stories. In addition to his fantasies about leprechauns and dragons, storyteller Jay O'Callahan now tells about his remarkable Uncle Joe and his experiences on a WWII aircraft carrier. Donald Davis still tells hilarious folktales about Jack in the Beanstalk, but he also moves audiences with stories of his wise and funny Aunt Laura. Jackie Torrence can still make the hair on the back of your neck stand up with a traditional ghost story like "The Bell Witch," but she is also likely to tell about her experience growing up. Family stories are bringing people together on a national scale.

I find that family stories bring us together in the classroom, too. When I bring a new group of tellers together (be they children, teachers, actors, librarians, or senior citizens), we almost always begin with our family stories. Before storytelling techniques, before story sources, before preparation strategies, before anything else that might explain *how* to tell stories, we find ourselves just jumping in and *doing* it. At the risk of sounding like a commercial for athletic shoes, "just do it" may be a good starting place for telling stories. There is a false assumption in the phrase, "I am learning to tell stories." It implies that there are two processes at work: learning to tell stories and then actually telling them. Yet we learn by doing. In other words, storytelling is a single process that involves learning and doing, an ongoing dance that continues to inform us throughout our lifetimes.

Students are often surprised to discover that one of their earliest assignments in my storytelling class, before they've learned anything about technique, is to tell a family story. "But I don't have any stories." That's a common refrain. Or, "I don't know how to tell stories; that's what you're supposed to teach me in this class." That's also an early response. Then the real work starts and the epiphanies begin.

Storytelling is a *folk* art form, meaning it is an art form of the people. It is part of the fabric of our lives. It is something that children do every day. At supper tables across the land every evening, storytelling is practiced. Grandparents recall their salad days, children dazzle us with the day's adventures, we build new relationships by sharing our past, and we lull our children to sleep—with storytelling. Telling stories is something we already do: "How was your weekend?" "Have you heard about the new boss?" "What happened in the fourth quarter?" We, the folk, tell stories all the time and therefore, at least a part of us already knows how to do this. And so, to learn how to tell stories, we embark on a journey of doing.

Rediscovering your family stories

As folk singer John McCutcheon writes:

> Now it don't take much, but you got to have some,
> The old ways help the new ways come.
> Just leave a little extra for the next in line,
> We're gonna need a little water from another time.*

The following discussion provides suggestions for rediscovering our own family stories. These are "pump priming" exercises; my hope is that they will help increase the flow of memory as stories begin to take shape.

1. The story of your name

All of us have stories to tell. In my own classes, I invite people to tell each other the story of their names. Questions help get everyone started.

- Were you named for someone? (A relative? A movie star? A character from a literary or religious work?)
- Do you know how and why your name was chosen?
- Does your name have meaning in another language?
- Does your name reflect a particular ethnicity?
- Was your family name changed at Ellis Island?
- Does your name adapt easily to nicknames?
- How have you felt about your name?
- Has your name changed?

Of course these questions don't have to be answered in any particular order, or even addressed at all. I usually list some questions as a means of getting people started and then invite them to tell each other informally about their names. In a small group, we may tell everyone; in a large group, we may turn

---

* "Water from Another Time," by John McCutcheon, copyright © 1985, Appalsongs (ASCAP), from the recording Gonna Rise Again (Rounder 222).

and tell a neighbor the story of our names. The conversations are lively—often there is laughter, occasionally tears. At a recent workshop, an elderly man told the story of how his name was changed when he was very young. He was very ill, near death in fact, and the Rabbi was called. The Rabbi pronounced his name dead, so that when the angel of death appeared, there would be no child by that name available. When the boy recovered later, he needed a new name to replace the one that had died. And so he was given a new name that he has carried with him to this very day. Although you may not have an unusual story like this to tell, often our names are the keepers of our stories. As we talk about them, we are storytelling before we know it.

2. When you were young...

Family stories can also be inspired by using a picture book such as one by Cynthia Rylant called *When I Was Young in the Mountains*. The charming text and illustrations invite us to remember a time when the author lived in rural West Virginia. It contains a series of vignettes, memories really, each beginning with the phrase, "When I was young in the mountains." Rylant shares memories of her father returning from work in the coal mines with his lips being the only part of him that wasn't covered with soot, her grandmother killing a black snake so long that the children could drape it across their shoulders for a photograph, memories of okra and outhouses, sweet milk and swimmin' holes. When I invite a group to explore this exercise I usually share enough of Rylant's book to give everyone the flavor of it, emphasizing the repetition of the phrase, "When I was young in the mountains."

Sometimes we discuss the book for a time, and then the fun really begins. I invite the group to split into pairs and find their own space in the room. One player begins by saying, "When I was young in ...," and inserts the name of a place she really knew when she was small. When I was young—in Pittsburgh, at the beach, on my grandpa's farm, at my daddy's office, in my granny's attic, etc. Then she continues with a brief memory of the place or the people who made it special. Then the second player responds, "When I was young ... The game continues back and forth, each player beginning with that phrase. The players are encouraged to get ideas from each other; one person's Fourth of July memory may trigger the long-forgotten picnic memory of another. After we have been playing for ten minutes or so, I invite the group to come together for discussion. The back-and-forth nature of the game as well as the ritualistic use of the repeated phrase make it a powerful tool for priming the pump of memory and beginning the flow of family stories. One woman commented, "I feel as if I know my story-partner better than colleagues I have worked with for twelve years."

3. Your family "roots"

Storytellers in many cultures are historians; chanted genealogies are found around the world as storytellers are entrusted with the responsibility of tending a people's roots. Personally, I never much cared for "so and so begat so and so who begat so and so," *ad infinitum*. But my feelings changed when my daughter was born. I wrote a storyteller's genealogy for her—a piece that I can say at her bedside now that she is small, and will use to teach her about her family when she grows older. The format is simple. Each phrase begins with "You are…"

> You are the great-great granddaughter of a woman who relished the language of Shakespeare, and who stood up to those who would censor the bawdy parts.
>
> And you are the great-granddaughter of an officer in the United States cavalry, who could ride standing up on two galloping horses at once.
>
> And you are the great-granddaughter of an orphan, who stood 4 feet, 11 inches tall, and raised 10 children.
>
> And you are the granddaughter of a woman who makes friends of strangers, and who keeps friends all her life.
>
> And you are the granddaughter of a most unlikely Ph.D., who has chosen to align himself with David, against Goliath.
>
> And you are the daughter of a woman who has appeared in the dreams of children, and who loves you with her every breath.
>
> And you are the daughter of a man who is the keeper of stories, and who loves you with his every breath.

This piece has become the catalyst for an exercise. I share it with children and then invite them to create six "I am…" statements about themselves and the people around them. Lots of variations are possible in this era of families that come in many shapes and sizes. "I am—the best friend of, the stepdaughter of, the brother of, the student of, the cousin of…" I invite the children to write the variations down, thinking poetically like storytellers rather than just including the facts. The group then comes together for a circle-telling of their work. One player starts by offering one of her phrases, beginning with the words, "I am the…" After her phrase she adds, "And…" which invites the next player to continue with one of his "I am" phrases. This continues around the circle until everyone has had an opportunity to contribute. My students have really enjoyed this, creating such gems as:

> "I am the great-granddaughter of a woman who believed that babies come from people's knees…."
>
> "I am the fiancée of a man who drove halfway across the country in his lemon of a car for a three-day weekend because he heard the sadness in my voice."
>
> "I am the grandson of a former nun who once slid down a bannister with a flask of gin in her garter."

Many follow-up activities are possible. One classroom was decorated by life-size tracings of students filled with "I am" statements. Family stories have grown in tribute to the characters and places mentioned poetically in the genealogies. Children and college students alike who have shared their storyteller's genealogies have discovered a paradox. We are each unique, yet we have so much in common. Our stories are ours alone and yet they are shared by many. There has never been anybody just like me and I am the same as those who have gone before. Perhaps this is what Joseph Campbell meant when he wrote,

Furthermore, we have not even to risk the journey alone, for the heroes of all time have gone before us. The labyrinth is thoroughly known. We have only to follow the thread of the hero path, and where we had thought to find an abomination, we shall find a god. And where we had thought to slay another, we shall slay ourselves. Where we had thought to travel outward, we shall come to the center of our own existence. And where we had thought to be alone, we will be with all the world.

Campbell, Joseph. 1988. *The Power of Myth*. New York: Doubleday, p. 151.

4. Your special place

Sometimes we can remember stories if we think about places that have been special to us. In my class, I invite players to remember a place that was important to them when they were younger. The place can be outdoors or indoors, a place they lived in for a long time or just visited for a short while. Often it is helpful to suggest that this was a special place where they felt secure.

The next step is to invite Player One to give her partner a tour of her remembered special place. The players are not to tell about the place, but rather they are to take their partner there—literally. Often I model this by taking hold of a volunteer's arm and saying, "Come with me, but duck your head as we go through this low doorway. We're going down into the cellar of the church. I'll show you what's underneath the sanctuary. Look over there; that's an unfinished wall of crumbling rock. It looks like the wall of a mystery-cave and in some places it goes way back into the darkness. We weren't supposed to come down here, but we did. It was great to be down here when the organ master was practicing upstairs. Come with me a little farther and I'll show you...." The players quickly get the idea. I send them off on their tours and the room is filled with simultaneous exploration of remembered places. Guests are encouraged to support their guides with questions that may make the space even more vivid, but they are not to add details of their own invention. The energy in the room grows as everyone talks at once, and typically pairs can be seen crawling or climbing or tightrope-walking as they get their bodies involved in the memories of these special places.

After five to ten minutes of the tour, guides are asked to bring the work to a close and guests are asked to convey to their guides some of the most vivid moments of their shared experience. Then the roles are reversed—guides become guests and guests become guides—and a second tour begins in a new place. Sometimes when the group is new to each other, we may come back in a circle and introduce each other by sharing a part of the tour. The places people go are wonderful:

- the grandmother's attic where the Victorian rocking horse was
- the vacant lot where the bulldozer was parked
- the summer house at the lake with the screened porch and the wicker furniture
- the basement with the furnace that looked and sounded like a monster
- the bell tower high above the church
- the fireplace with the mantle covered with greeting cards

Stories are associated with places. From the memory of place often comes the memory of character and incident, the people we knew and the things that happened. At a recent summer workshop, a player's special place evoked the near-forgotten memory of an important character—a dog who shared childhood with him. From our places come our stories.

There are many approaches to remembering stories by recalling places. Author Sam Keene invites participants to get down on the floor with butcher paper and draw the floor plan of the house they grew up in. He encourages as much detail as the players can muster, and stories flow from the sharing of the plans. Storyteller Lynn Rubright invites people to close their eyes while she uses guided imagery to help them remember a special place, and then asks them to fill a blank page with notes of their memories. I like inviting people to give each other tours because of the kinesthetic involvement, allowing the body to remember as the players move through space. Stories emerge as a player pets the remembered image of an animal or points to the place where a tree grew.

A family story in the making

As I suggest in the first chapter, we're all storytellers. Ethan Collins, at age four, is the youngest teller to be included in this book. Here's a story we shared one rainy afternoon.

Photo by Dawn Murray

Dad: Ethan, this is a story just for you. We'll make it up together. Once upon a time at the base of a great mountain lived a ... (Each set of ellipses indicates a place where I paused, signaling to Ethan that he could add his ideas here.)

Ethan: A Sharptooth! AArrrrr! (He stood up on the easy chair and with his arms above him made a great growl.)

Dad: Yes, there was a Sharptooth, a great big Sharptooth and his teeth were like ....

Ethan: Knifes!

Dad: Right! Long, long teeth as sharp as knives. And his legs were as strong as ...

Ethan: Oaks!

Dad: Right! He had great powerful legs as strong as tree trunks. And Ethan, how did he walk? (Ethan stood up now and began to stomp great giant steps around the living room as he growled and growled.) All day he would do this, until one day he had a problem, and his problem was ...

Ethan: He couldn't tie his shoes.

Dad: Oh, that's right. He couldn't tie his shoes. He would growl and try to reach his shoes, but with his little bitty front paws, he couldn't tie them. And how did this make him feel?

Ethan: Mad, mad, mad!

Dad: Ooh, that's right. He was so angry because he wanted to be able to tie his shoes. And the Sharptooth would say, "Everybody else around me seems to be able to tie shoes, but I can't do it, and it makes me angry. Rrrarrrrrr!" Well just then, who was listening in the bushes?

Ethan: Sarah.

Dad: That's right, Sarah was ... who's Sarah?

Ethan: A nice dinosaur, a really nice triceratops.

Dad: Right. And Sarah came out and she said, "Sharptooth, your shoes are untied. Would you like help?" And Sharptooth said ...

Ethan: No! No, no, no!

Dad: And he began to stomp around until Sarah ran away. He stomped and stomped and stomped until, all of a sudden, he tripped over his own shoelace. Down he fell! And guess what happened?

Ethan: He bumped out a tooth.

Dad: That's right. He bumped out a tooth and it really, really hurt, and he cried and cried and cried. And that night, he ...

Ethan: Put his tooth under the pillow and the tooth fairy came.

Dad: That's right, the tooth fairy came, and she left him a note and the note said, "Everybody needs a little help sometimes. Ask your friends." Did Sharptooth have any friends?

Ethan: No.

Dad: But he was crying and crying, and he was sitting outside his cave when, up in the trees, who did he hear?

Ethan: Pterodactyl.

Dad: That's right, he heard Pterodactyl, who was up in the tree. And Pterodactyl said, "What's wrong?"
"Grrrrarr! I don't have any friends."
"Well, that's because you're so mean."
Sharptooth said, "I'm not mean."
He said, "Well, you stomp on dinosaurs' homes."
"So?"
"And, you eat up other dinosaurs."
"So?"
"And, you roar so loud it scares everybody."
"So?"
"So, that's mean."

"Oh ... oh."
"Maybe if you weren't so mean, you'd have some friends."
Now, what do you suppose the Sharptooth dinosaur did to get some friends?

Ethan: He got his truck.

Dad: He got his truck? Tell me about his truck.

Ethan: It was a dump truck.

Dad: His dump truck!

Ethan: It was a big dump truck, and he could drive it. Vrrrrrm. Vrrmmm. (Ethan sat in his chair and showed me steering wheel hands and a stick shift.)

Dad: I see, I see. And what did he do with his truck?

Ethan: It was a dump truck. He dumped out some rocks so everyone could see.

Dad: Wow, Ethan! And what did the other dinosaurs say?

Ethan: "Can we have a turn?"

Dad: They wanted a turn! And what did Sharptooth say?

Ethan: He said, "Okay."

Dad: He said, "Okay." Wow. And so, that afternoon, Sarah and the Pterodactyl, they all had a turn driving the big dump truck and dumping out the boulders. But then they noticed that poor Sharptooth was rubbing his mouth and saying, "Ohhh!" And Pterodactyl said, "I know how to get some medicine for the place where your tooth came out." And Ethan, guess what he made medicine out of?

Ethan: Flowers!

Dad: That's right. He cut some flowers and he ground them up and he flew up to Sharptooth's mouth. And Sharptooth opened up his mouth and the Pterodactyl reached inside where all those sharp teeth were and Sarah said, "Be careful! He'll eat you!"
And Pterodcatyl said, "Are you going to eat me?"
And Sharptooth said ...

Ethan: "No!"

Dad: And so, Pterodactyl put the flowers on the place where the tooth came out, and almost immediately, Sharptooth felt better. And when he looked down toward the ground, he saw that Sarah had tied his shoes. His shoes weren't untied anymore.

Ethan: He said, "Thank you."

Dad: And that's the story of how Sharptooth discovered his friends.

Ethan and I both applauded. He gave me a big hug and ran off to play. It was a satisfying time for both of us. And the power came not in the moments when I was speaking, but in the silences. The real magic happened when I paused to let my son contribute to the story—to make this story uniquely his own. Although this tale may not stand on its literary merits, it is important for the bond it creates and celebrates between a father and son. Ethan told me about things that are important to him during these magical preschool years. He told about tying shoes and making friends and sharing toys and losing teeth. Such were the concerns of his world on that particular day, and they found their way into a story. He became my teacher, and the story became a way for us to enjoy and know each other better. As parents, of course we love our children. But how do we show our love? How is the love we feel made manifest in the rapid-paced world in which we live? Sometimes, the answer can be found in the sharing of a story.

Conclusion

Livo and Rietz (1986) describe the storyteller as "the one who can take us safely from one time, place and reality to another and back again." Storytelling involves a teller transporting an audience to places and people she knows well, whether they are actual or fictitious. Students are invited to tell all stories (be they family tales, folktales, or literary stories) as if they were memories of characters, locales, and events they have encountered and remember vividly. And they are invited to treat audiences, large or small, as they did the partner who has shared the house tour with them. (See page 28.) The storyteller does not perform to an abstract fourth wall but makes eye contact as she shares her stories with an engaged audience. The extraordinary power of storytelling occurs at the confluence of a story, an audience, and a teller. As the following Venn diagram illustrates, storytelling is synergistic. The story itself is co-created as the teller and audience imagine together in the communal dream that is storytelling. The coming together of a carefully chosen story, a heartfelt telling, and an engaged audience is called enchantment.

This Venn diagram illustrates that storytelling is synergistic.

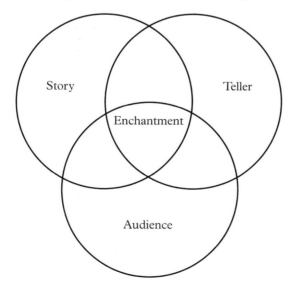

FAVORITE FAMILY STORIES TO SHARE

Ackerman, Karen. 1988. *Song and Dance Man.* New York: Alfred Knopf.

Bunting, Eve. 1988. *How Many Days to America?* New York: Clarion Books.

Cameron, Ann. 1986. *More Stories Julian Tells.* New York: Knopf.

Cameron, Ann. 1981. *The Stories Julian Tells.* New York: Pantheon.

Capote, Truman. 1985. *I Remember Grandpa.* Atlanta: Peachtree Publishers.

Garcia, Richard. 1987. *My Aunt Otilia's Spirits.* Chicago: Children's Book Press.

Greenfield, Eloise. 1988. *Grandpa's Face.* New York: Putnam & Grosset.

Hoffman, Mary. 1991. *Amazing Grace.* New York: Dial Books for Young Readers.

Howard, Elizabeth Fitzgerald. 1991. *Aunt Flossie's Hats (and Crab Cakes Later).* New York: Clarion Books.

Khalsa, Dayal Kaur. 1986. *Tales of a Gambling Grandma.* New York: Clarkson N. Potter.

Lasky, Kathryn. 1988. *Sea Swan.* New York: MacMillan.

Martin, Bill Jr., and Jon Archambault. 1987. *Knots on a Counting Rope.* New York: Bantam Doubleday Dell.

Palmer, Kate Salley. 1991. *A Gracious Plenty.* New York: Simon & Schuster.

Polacco, Patricia. 1988. *The Keeping Quilt.* New York: Simon & Schuster.

Ringgold, Faith. 1991. *Tar Beach.* New York: Crown Publishers.

Rylant, Cynthia. 1985. *The Relatives Came.* New York: Bradbury Press.

_____. 1982. *When I Was Young in the Mountains.* New York: E. P. Dutton.

Shecter, Ben. 1989. *Grandma Remembers.* New York: Harper & Row.

Stoltz, Mary. 1988. *Storm in the Night.* New York: Harper & Row.

Willard, Nancy. 1990. *The High Rise Glorious Skittle Skat Roarious Sky Pie Angel Food Cake.* San Francisco: Harcourt Brace Jovanovich.

SUGGESTED READINGS

Akeret, Robert U. 1991. *Family Tales, Family Wisdom: How to Gather the Stories of a Lifetime and Share Them with Your Family.* New York: William Morrow and Company.
Sheds light on discovering the role family stories play in the shaping of the self.

Allison, Christine. 1987. *I'll Tell You a Story, I'll Sing You a Song*. New York: Dell Publishing.

A parent's guide to the fairytales, fables, songs, and rhymes of childhood. Excellent sourcebook of songs and stories with solid suggestions for learning and telling stories. Especially good for those who don't think they are the theatrical type.

Collins, Chase. 1992. *Tell Me a Story: Creating Bedtime Tales Your Children Will Dream On*. New York: Houghton Mifflin Co.

Especially encouraging for those who want to make up stories for their children.

Greene, Bob, and D. G. Fulford. 1992. *To Our Children's Children: Preserving Family Histories for Generations to Come*. New York: Doubleday.

A marvelous book of questions to prime the pump of memory for family stories.

Helm-Meade, Erica. 1995. *Tell It by Heart*. Chicago: Open Court Publishing Co.

Beautifully written, this book explores the role of stories in the lives of women.

McAdams, Dan P. 1993. *Stories We Live By: Personal Myths and the Making of the Self*. New York: William Morrow and Co.

A psychological study that examines the role of family stories throughout the lifespan. An insightful resource.

Pellowski, Anne. 1987. *The Family Storytelling Handbook: How to Use Stories, Anecdotes, Rhymes, Handkerchiefs, Paper and Other Objects to Enrich Your Family Traditions*. New York: Macmillan.

Bedtimes, car trips, and family reunions all provide occasion for storytelling as this book helps tellers find and share their family lore.

Meet the storyteller...
Nancy Donoval

Nancy Donoval, who holds an MFA in directing, is a full-time professional storyteller and executive director of the Wild Onion Storytelling Festival, Chicago's premier storytelling celebration.

Q: You're a professional storyteller.

A: Yes.

Q: Will you tell us about the kind of work you do?

A: I perform in schools and libraries, for professional groups and women's clubs, and at storytelling festivals. As an artist-in-residence, I work with students as they are creating/writing/telling their own stories. I focus on different aspects of that process depending on what it is that the sponsor wants. We could be dealing with creative writing or public speaking or curriculum-based work like the Greek myths. Story and storytelling fits in most any curriculum with any age group. During my favorite 24 hours as a storyteller, I was in Wisconsin one afternoon telling dragon stories to six-year-olds in a park. Then the next morning, I was back in Chicago in a courtroom telling stories to a trial law class. They'd hired me to take a case study and turn it into two stories, one making each side look right. I've always felt those two jobs illustrate the range of what story can be. I also teach storytelling classes and give workshops on various storytelling skills. Because of my background as a director, I like working as a private coach for other storytellers to help them to get their stories out. Sort of like a birth coach or midwife. A lot of hard work and sweat and it can be messy, but boy, is it worth it.

Q: I've heard you tell some wonderful folktales and literary stories, but, for today, let's talk about the autobiographical stories that you tell. Why do you tell autobiographical or family stories?

A: My goal doing an autobiographical story is not to have anyone say afterward, "Oh, isn't her life interesting?" or "Oh, wasn't that sad for her?" or "My goodness, she's funny." That's not the point. When I tell a story from my life, it's because I want to touch the stories in other people's lives that they have tucked away or not thought about or thought, "Well, this happened to me, but it's not something I could ever talk to anyone about," or "That was just this goofy thing that happened and no one would be interested in that." I think of telling autobiographical stories as a way of opening doors to stories that the listeners have in their lives and giving them permission to embrace those stories.

I tell a story about my father that celebrates his life while also dealing with his death when I was fifteen. It weaves back and forth between his final week and my memories of childhood with him. People come up to me afterwards, but it's very rare that someone will talk to me about the story that I just told. They tell me about their own fathers or mothers, their own childhoods, their own experiences. I had someone apologize once that he'd missed the last half of my story because he was lost in funny, happy child-hood memories of his sister who had died recently—stuff he hadn't thought about in years. I can only take that as a compliment.

The nicest thing anyone ever said to me after hearing my dad's story was "You just told the story of my life. My father died when I was sixteen and I've missed him every day of my life but I've never told anyone about him. It's too late for my children but I'm going home and gathering up my grandchildren and telling them about the wonderful man who was their great-grandfather." Here it is, 60 years later and she's never talked about her dad! And even though she thinks her children are too old to care, *I* know that while she's talking to the grandkids, their parents will be sneaking out from the kitchen or office or den to hear about their grandfather for the first time. There is so much joy in telling stories about those we love who have made us who we are. So, what I really work for in stories is to find the moments we recognize so well that we laugh when we think of them, and we feel our hearts get bigger because the emotion is so big, and the tender-ness is so great that we're not sure whether we're going to laugh or cry.

Q: Sometimes I do both. I laugh and cry.

A: Good. You know, we have these human experiences and we don't talk about them. We go through our lives so quickly and we don't slow down to let events ripple through us, to really process them. And what I'm trying to do in autobiographical stories is to say to people, "Slow down. Slow down and really see your life." I'm working on a new story, and one section of it is about my first kiss as a teenager. And it's very funny and very painful and very sad and very silly and everything that being a teenager is. I just look at it and I think, "Wow, that's all of my teen years in one event." But I'm not telling it to say, "Look at this, *my* teen years were like this." I look for what is universal in the experience. And that's the way I can tell stories about things that are still very resonant for me.

Q: How do you do that? How do you talk about things that are obviously so personal and potentially hard to talk about?

A: Stories can be told at different stages of emotional readiness to different audiences and for different purposes. If you're trying to tell a personal story to another family member who you've never really talked with about it, try-ing to formulate it in your mind for one-to-one communication that's one thing. If you're telling a highly emotional, resonant, difficult story in a self-help group, and you want to use it maybe to illustrate something that's a pat-tern in your life, or maybe it's a story that you've held inside that just needs to come out and be heard, go for it! That's fine. And if you break down in tears in the middle of it, that's okay, it's appropriate. But if you want to make a story from your life into a piece of public art, then you need to have done the emotional work beforehand, so that you can be telling it as a gift to open doors for the listeners, not as a moment of group therapy for yourself. If it is too hard to talk about, then it is not time to tell that story and it won't come out right. So don't tell the story. Wait until you have the distance and the healing or whatever it is you need to tell the story more for others than for yourself. If you can't talk about it without crying, if you can't tell it without being filled with a great rage or bitterness toward someone or something, then it's not ready to be told as a public piece of art.

Part of your job as a storyteller is to keep your audience safe. If you are going to lead them into the dark, which is an important place to go, you have to bring them out into the light. It is essential, if you are going to tell a story with a lot of darkness in it, to balance it with light all the way through. It can be humor, or beauty, or forgiveness. Light comes in many forms. But if you can't find it for yourself, you can't find it for the audience.

Q: An autobiographical story doesn't have to be dark, or serious, or heavy to be worth telling, does it?

A: Oh my goodness, no! No. There are so many experiences and emotions in life, and stories can celebrate them all. We *need* to celebrate them all. Love and laughter, friendship and foolishness. There is a great joy in telling true stories that celebrate what is universal about being human.

Q: In addition to being a storyteller yourself, you also teach others to find their own family stories. Is that right?

A: In the adult education classes I teach, I have students in their 20s and in their 70s and one of their favorite parts of the class is telling family stories. Some of them tell me that they rediscover parts of their childhood in a way that they never would have even thought of doing. It's great fun for them and for me.

Q: Children can tell family stories as well, can't they?

A: Last fall, I did a project that I loved. I was doing a residency for third-, fourth-, and fifth-graders on storytelling and creative writing, and the first week I was there, we had five elders from their community come in. It was kind of like *This Is Your Life* or *What's My Line*. We had our panel of elders and the kids and I worked on questions the day before. What kind of questions could they ask these elders to elicit stories? The kids would want to ask, "Did you like your teachers?" and I would suggest we rephrase the question to be, "Would you tell me about one of your teachers you really liked?" You need to move away from "yes and no" questions to get a story. And part of what I was trying to teach was how to use questioning for their own creative writing skills. They would not only be able to use these interviewing techniques on other people, but at some time, they would be able to turn the questioning on themselves to be able to get or expand a story that way.

Anyway, the children worked on their questions and the elders came; they ranged in age from 27 to 85, and they were all from the kids' community. For example, one of the elder's grandfathers used to own the land that the school was built on. For the most part, children don't have much contact with older people and their stories, so there's this moment of everyone feeling like they're in a foreign country and not knowing what language to speak. I had to be really clear with the elders that they had to let the kids' questions guide what to talk about. What the elders thought would be interesting and what the kids really *were* interested in might be different. One of the women was 85 and a retired physical education teacher. So, one boy had a question on his list which we had adjusted from, "Did you like sports when you were young?" to "What kind of sports did you like when you were young?" Since she had been a gym teacher he asked her. She was this itsy, bitsy little woman and you could see that none of the kids expected a very exciting answer. Well, it turns out that her father was the pitcher for the Chicago Red Stockings, which is the team that became the White Sox, and she was the bat girl for the team. She told us about how they only had two balls and two bats, so she had to learn how to run really fast because every time both balls were out of play, the game would stop. And because she learned to move so fast, she became a speed skater and won the Silver Skates here in Chicago and qualified for the Olympics. After that she was a professional tennis player. All the kids' jaws were bouncing off the floor.

It was like that with all the elders, these jewels were just falling out of their mouths. And they didn't have to be sports heroes for the children to love their stories. One man told this hilarious story about being a volunteer fireman. The story involved a burning onion storage shed and one of the firemen falling into the lower level of an outhouse that had burned down behind the shed. He hadn't noticed because the of the burning onion smell. The kids just loved it! They ate it up. The school counselor was in that session observing the residency and she said that there were kids there that she had never seen really interest in anything who just came alive listening to these stories. And, you know, one of the wonderful things that came from that was some of the kids decided to interview some of the elders further and write a biographical story about them for their creative writing project. Some of the students went home and talked to their own grandparents and asked them questions and came back and told their stories. But the sense of connections between the generations! Also, so many kids would say about themselves, "Well, I don't have any stories. My life is boring." As if their lives didn't have value. And one of the things that I wanted very much from the elders was stories to show that "Everybody's stories are as important and worthwhile as any story we read in a book or see on TV. Our stories have value too. *Your* stories have value.

Note: For information about her performances, workshops, audiocassettes, and the Wild Onion Festival, Ms. Donoval can be reached at (847) 869-0807.

CHAPTER 4

· · · · · · · · · · · · · · · · · · · ·

Going to the Well:
Choosing Stories for Telling

Every good story has mystery—not the puzzle kind, but the mystery
of allurement.

Eudora Welty

T HERE IS an Irish legend of a man who could not tell stories. His name was Brian, you see, and he was but a humble weaver of baskets. As he was gathering rods one day, a terrible wind arose and a blow to the head knocked him out. When he awoke, he was in the home of a kindly old man and woman, who fed him by their fire. He thanked them for their kindness and offered to repay them. "We'll accept no money," they replied simply. "Just treat us to a story." "A story?" he laughed, "Oh, I'm no storyteller. I don't know anything about telling stories." But the elderly couple insisted. "What?" they asked, "an Irishman who can't tell stories? Surely you're foolin' with us now. A tale of the fairies, or of the kings, maybe one of your own making—that's all we ask."

Brian grew flustered. "I'm just a maker of baskets. I don't know the first thing about telling stories. I have no tale to tell. And I wouldn't know where to begin if I had one. I'm sorry to disappoint you." Brian looked at his shoes, which were in need of repair. The old man rubbed his bald head. "No tale to tell." There was mystery (or was it mischief?) in his voice. "No tale at all, you say?" "Now don't be too hard on the young man," said his wife as she picked up a wooden bucket. "You can repay us by filling this at the well."

Brian took the bucket and started down the path. The elderly couple stood framed in their doorway, watching him go into the night. Then they turned to each other and smiled with their eyes.

Brian was at the well when a terrible wind came up. He was tossed into the air and landed outside a wakehouse. This wake had no music, the people explained, because the fiddler hadn't arrived. Suddenly a beautiful girl with long, dark hair and green eyes exclaimed, "Why, it's Brian, the finest fiddler in all the land!" The fiddle and bow were placed in his hands. Before he could explain that he knew nothing about music, he began to play. Such music it was; the people danced through the night. Word came that the priest could not come, and everyone grew worried, for it was time to put this body in the ground. "Not to worry!" cried the green-eyed girl, "Brian is with us—the finest priest in all the land!" Before he could explain that he knew nothing of this, the robes had been placed over his shoulders. He opened his mouth to speak, and out came the finest funeral you ever heard.

After the service, the pallbearers lifted the body to their shoulders. Three of the men were the same height, but the fourth was a head taller, and the body kept sliding to the ground. "Oh, if only we had a surgeon to make me the size of my friends," sighed the tallest. "Not to worry," said the girl, kissing Brian on the cheek, "We have the finest surgeon in all the land right here with us." Brian tried to tell them that he knew nothing about medicine, but the people knew by now to pay no attention to his protests. The scalpel was placed in his hand, and to the cheers of the crowd, Brian cut enough bone from below the big man's knees to make him the same height as the other three. As the group marched to the graveside, Brian heard his name on everyone's lips. Fiddler, priest, surgeon—such a man they had never met.

As Brian was climbing over the wall to the graveyard, the great wind came up again. Brian was thrown high into the air. He was alone when he landed, lying next to the well. Where the beautiful girl with the dark hair and green eyes had once been, there was now only an empty wooden bucket.

Brian filled the bucket and ran back to the home of the elderly couple. The story poured out of him as his words tried to keep up with his memory. The night didn't last as long as his story; he finished to the accompaniment of morning birdsong. The old man and the old woman stood framed in their doorway as they bade Brian farewell. "When others ask you for a story," they cried, "You tell them that one!" And that's just what he did. Many times he told it, and other tales followed that first story. Soon people exclaimed, "Why, it's Brian, the finest teller in all the land!" Brian lived well after that, and he never made another basket.

I like to share that story at the beginning of a workshop, and teachers often tell me they identify with Brian. "I'm no storyteller. I have no story to tell, and wouldn't know where to begin even if I had one." Where to begin. That always seems to be the hardest part. Mostly, I just send them to the well and, like the old man and woman, I never cease to be amazed at what they come back with. This chapter is all about going to the well, finding stories to share with others.

Fortunately for us all, the well is deep. Folktales, fairytales, picture books, ghost stories, histories, literature, family stories—there is never a shortage of material. The challenge lies in selecting the right story. I suggest three common-sense considerations when choosing a story:

1. You as a teller.
2. Your students as listeners.
3. The occasion of this particular telling.

You as a teller

Actually, I don't usually choose stories at all. The stories choose me. I read ten to twelve stories for each one I choose to tell. My initial impressions of stories might be, "interesting," "cute," "clever," "no, thank you." And then a story seems to jump out and say, "Tell me. I'm the story for you. Tell me." To say no to a story like this doesn't do any good. It will haunt you until you tell it. This process is obviously highly intuitive. I used to be embarrassed by that, but I have grown to trust it. Share the stories that speak to you. Often I share stories that make me laugh out loud. Sometimes I find myself drawn to stories that contain thrilling sequences of suspense. Characters I can care about and identify with are important to me, and I believe all great stories have love in them. Powerful imagery and colorful language may draw me to a story. I tend to be drawn to stories that make me feel something strongly, and to stories that affirm the dignity and mystery of the world we live in. I can't always put into words just why I feel connected to a particular story, but I share the ones I am compelled to tell, the ones that say, "Tell me."

I encourage tellers, "Listen to the stories that speak to you and share the ones you like." A favorite story your grandpa used to tell you about the old country, a ghost story that gave you goosebumps at camp, a picture book that tickles you, a true story about an important time in your own life—stories you care about will tell beautifully. But be warned. It is a bad idea to tell a story you don't care about but think your listeners will like. Trying to please your audience with material you don't like is always dangerous, especially if you are telling to children. This condescending attitude has led to the proliferation of commercial drivel that floods the airwaves on Saturday mornings. While it is a wonderful experience to hear a teller share a story she genuinely loves, it is painful to watch someone pander to an audience without having any connection to the story itself. So, when choosing a story, the first consideration is *you,* the teller. Whenever possible, allow for the richness that occurs when you share a story that already has spoken to you.

Your students as listeners

The second consideration when choosing a story is your listeners. Although sharing a story you care about is important, storytelling does not involve a self-indulgent disregard for the audience. Storytelling is connecting—teller to tale, then teller to audience, and finally audience to story. A good teller chooses a story as a gift for people he cares about. A tale that is popular in storytelling circles illustrates this:

> I was working in central Africa as a Peace Corps volunteer when the trucks rolled into our village. On the side of the trucks were the words "RURAL ELECTRIFICATION." Many of the elders spoke out against the changes this new electricity would bring, but Nkundi, the wise old storyteller of the village, pointed out that change need not always be feared. Soon there was light even in the middle of the night. Electricity had not been in the village long before a television set arrived. It was quickly installed in a gathering place for all to see. When I went to the storytelling circle, I saw the television on top of Nkundi's stool, surrounded by listeners agape with curiosity. Nkundi stood alone away from the circle.
>
> I wasn't able to return to the circle for a couple of weeks, but when I did, things had changed again. The television set had been moved to the side; it was covered with a cloth. Nkundi had resumed his place on the storytelling stool and again was surrounded by listeners. No longer were their faces filled with curiosity; now they were alive with wonder. Nkundi paused as the children laughed, and I asked a small boy, "Is the television set broken?" "No," he said and went back to listening. Again I tapped him. "What," he said, clearly annoyed at the prospect of missing any of the story, which I knew he had heard before. I asked, "The television set ... doesn't the television set know more stories than Nkundi?" The boy thought for a moment. "Yes, the television knows more stories. But my storyteller," he smiled a

gap-toothed grin, "My storyteller knows me." And again the child left me for the world of the story.

Part of the enormous power of storytelling in schools results from the fact that teacher-tellers, like the wise Nkundi, know their listeners. This truth allows us to choose stories we love that will be especially appropriate for the needs and concerns of the students we teach. Again and again I encourage teachers to discover their own wisdom, for they know their specific listeners better than any outside experts do.

When my wife and I were expecting our second child, I created stories for my daughter about new babies. We created a story together about two stuffed animals who wanted to run away when they learned the girl they lived with was going to have a new baby brother. Certain they would soon be thrown into the trash, Buster and Woof made plans to leave forever. The girl caught up with them at the end of the driveway just as they were about to pedal away on the Bigwheel. "Hey! Where do you two think you're going?" My daughter loved that line. And then she would help convince the two that they would always be special, even when the new baby arrived. That story brought us laughter and encouragement at a time of uncertainty. She asked for it again and again, but doesn't need it now that her new brother is really here. It is the kind of story that can be told only by one who knows the listener.

The occasion of this particular telling

The third consideration for those choosing stories is the occasion for the telling, the specific time and place and circumstance of this particular need for story. Knowing the students' curriculum, the season of the year, even the place in the day can influence the choice of story. Stories can enrich the unit on Africa. Stories can bring to life characters studied in history; the struggles of Edison and Magellan and Kennedy and Galileo become exciting in the hands of the teller. Black History Month is richer with tales of Harriet Tubman and Sojourner Truth. Women's History Month is richer with tales of Susan B. Anthony, Eleanor Roosevelt, and our own mothers. Stories can add spooky magic to the excitement of Halloween, romance to Valentine's Day, and joy to the birthday child who is allowed to choose the story of the day. Stories can bring quiet closure to the end of a hectic day.

A saying in the theater for those who would direct plays is, "Ninety percent of directing is correcting the mistakes we made at casting." And, as the director must choose his players wisely, so too must we select our stories with care. And so we go to the well. We choose stories for telling, keeping in mind ourselves, our listeners, and the occasion of this telling.

Twenty terrific anthologies of tellable tales

- Ed Brody, Jay Goldspinner, Katie Green, Rona Leventhal, and John Porcino, eds. 1992. *Spinning Tales and Weaving Hope: Stories of Peace, Justice, and the Environment.* Philadelphia: New Society Publishers.
- Richard Chase. 1948. *Grandfather Tales.* Cambridge, MA: Houghton Mifflin.
- Richard Chase. 1943. *The Jack Tales.* Cambridge, MA: Houghton Mifflin.
- Harold Courlander and George Herzog. 1947. *The Cow-Tail Switch and Other West African Stories.* New York: Holt, Rinehart and Winston.
- Pleasant de Spain. 1993. *Thirty-three Multicultural Tales to Tell.* Little Rock, AR: August House.
- Linda Goss and Marian E. Barnes. 1989. *Talk that Talk: An Anthology of African-American Stories.* New York: Simon and Schuster.
- Virginia Hamilton. 1992. *Many Thousand Gone: African-Americans from Slavery to Freedom.* New York: Knopf.
- Virginia Hamilton. 1985. *The People Could Fly: American Black Folktales.* New York: Knopf.
- David Holt and Bill Mooney. 1994. *Ready to Tell Tales.* Little Rock, AR: August House.
- Jennifer Justice, ed. 1992. *The Ghost and I: Scary Stories for Participatory Telling.* Cambridge, MA: Yellow Moon Press.
- Margaret Read MacDonald. 1992. *Peace Tales: World Folktales to Talk About.* North Haven, CT: Linnet Books.
- Margaret Read MacDonald. 1986. *Twenty Tellable Tales: Audience Participation Folktales from Around the World.* New York: H. W. Wilson.
- Teresa Miller, compiler, with assistance from Anne Pellowski, Ed. by Norma Livo. 1988. *Joining In: An Anthology of Audience Participation Stories and How to Tell Them.* Cambridge, MA: Yellow Moon Press.
- Ethel J. Phelps. 1981. *The Maid of the North: Feminist Folktales from Around the World.* New York: Holt, Rinehart and Winston.
- Robert D. San Souci, reteller. 1987. *Short and Shivery: Thirty Chilling Tales.* Garden City, NJ: Doubleday.
- Peninnah Schram. 1987. *Jewish Stories One Generation Tells Another.* Northvale, NJ: Aronson.
- Alvin Schwartz. 1984. *More Scary Stories to Tell in the Dark.* New York: Harper and Row.
- Jimmy Neil Smith, ed. 1988. *Homespun: Tales from America's Favorite Storytellers.* New York: Crown.
- Diane Wolkstein. 1978. *The Magic Orange Tree and Other Haitian Folktales.* New York: Knopf.
- Jane Yolen. 1986. *Favorite Folktales from Around the World.* New York: Pantheon.

SUGGESTED READINGS

Allison, Christine. 1987. *I'll Tell You a Story, I'll Sing You a Song.* New York: Dell.
A parents' guide to the fairytales, fables, songs, and rhymes of childhood.

Bauer, Caroline. 1977. *Handbook for Storytellers.* Chicago: American Language Association.
First published in 1942, this has become a classic resource. It includes excellent information on the history of storytelling, and wonderful stories for telling.

Hamilton, Martha, and Weiss, Mitch. 1990. *Children Tell Stories.* New York: Richard C. Owen.
Contains twenty-five short, tellable stories and a bibliography of tales especially appropriate for student tellers.

MacDonald, Margaret. 1986. *Twenty Tellable Tales.* New York: H. W. Wilson.
Audience participation folktales for the beginning storyteller.

Pellowski, Anne. 1984. *The Story Vine: A Source Book of Unusual and Easy to Tell Stories from Around the World.* New York: Collier Books.
This unusual collection of stories asks the teller to use string, nesting dolls, drawings, sand paintings, or musical instruments to tell.

Sawyer, Ruth. 1962. *The Way of the Storyteller.* 2d ed. New York: Viking.
An inspirational source, this book (originally published in 1942) endures as a classic in the field. Contains beautiful but challenging stories for telling.

Weaver, Mary C., ed. 1994. *Tales as Tools: The Power of Story in the Classroom.* Jonesborough, TN: National Storytelling Press.
Contains exceptionally complete bibliographies.

Yolen, Jane. 1986. *Favorite Folktales from Around the World.* New York: Pantheon.
Exceptionally rich anthology of beautiful world tales organized by theme.

Meet the storyteller...

Syd Lieberman

Syd Lieberman, a high school English teacher, is now a professional storyteller of national prominence. He lives with his wife in Evanston, Illinois.

Q: Syd, begin by telling me what a professional storyteller does.

A: Well, there are several things. First, in the school setting. I go in and tell stories to students. In addition, there are other things that the school will have you do—there's teaching teachers about storytelling, teaching teachers about ways to use storytelling, teaching teachers about ways to use storytelling in connection with their given discipline. I like to connect it with writing. I think the connections with reading are obvious, and I think there are some connections with writing that people don't know about. I do workshops with kids doing the same thing—connecting storytelling with writing—trying to turn them into storytellers. I also emphasize storytelling's relationship to reading.

Q: Can you illustrate that?

A: Sure. I'm in an inner-city library in St. Louis, in a very poor section of town. I'm doing a show for third- and fourth-graders. The kids are having a great time. The show finishes, the kids go to leave, and one kid walks up to me with a teacher. He looks at me and says, "Where'd you get those stories?" I said, "Books." We're in the middle of the library, and he says, "Books?" I said, "Yeah, books." He's looking at me like I speak a foreign language. I said, "Which story did you like the best?" So he tells the story. I said, "You know what? It's a book. I bet the library has it." The teacher grabbed the kid, and they took off. About three minutes later the kid walks back, holding the book, with a smile on his face. The teacher just looked at me. There's a kid who somehow never understood what was in a book, the pleasure you could get out of one.

Q: What else does a professional storyteller do besides go into schools?

A: Well, there are many interesting applications that I have been finding now that I am out there doing. I'll give you some examples. A man (who's connected with a clinic in LaCrosse, Wisconsin) saw me storytell, and when the story was over, he said, "You know the doctors are faced with such stress in their lives. They're faced with death, and there's a tendency to lose humanity in that situation. We're fighting all the time to try to keep them relating to their patients as people and not just as things, not just 'the gall bladder in 209.'" He said, "I don't know what I want you to do, but I think one of the answers is in story, and I want to hire you." How's that for vision?

We talked over the year, and my suggestion was "storyteller as caregiver." So that's what we did. The three-hour workshop showed how to find storytelling in your own life. I heard story after story testifying to story's power to heal and transform, the need to tell stories from trouble, the need to tell these stories and somehow transform your trouble, face your trouble. You live through something that's horrible and a few months later you're laughing about it. So how does that happen? It happens through story. Once it becomes a story out there, it's out there, and once it's out there, you can take one step away from it. Once you take one step away from it, you can get perspective on it.

Q: And that's healing?

A: Yes, and that's healing. You can find laughter. And the laughter is a laughter at the human condition. It's a laughter that says, "Ha! Look at this, will ya? Look what life is about." It is a laughter which is wonderful because it takes you as the storyteller and puts you with the audience saying, "God, look what's going on here in life."

Q: Is that what you mean when you talk about a relationship with your audience?

A: Yes, in a way the relationship happens because a storyteller has to connect with the crowd he's talking to. And I think the group has to know that you care about them, that you're not just up there performing. I really mean that. You go to see plays and you see wonderful actors. It's a wonderful experience to watch an actor work and really know he's enjoying his work. That's an extra, added treasure. That's fun. But I think a storyteller not only enjoys the story, but he has to enjoy the audience. The audience has to know this, that you're enjoying the story with them. And that it's important. If a story happens, it happens between the audience and the storyteller. If they're not with you, then it's not going to happen. I've worked with the clergy, lawyers, hospice workers. It's always the same—you've got to make this connection, this relationship.

Q: Let's talk for a moment about personal narratives. I know you tell a lot of your own stories. How can we, as people who have lived our own stories, gain access to them and share them?

A: The first thing is that people have to know that they have them—that they have stories. They don't know. We gobble our existence so quickly, things are going so fast. We hardly have time to reflect on what's happening to us. But we all have stories that will make us laugh, that will make us cry, that will make us think. Kids have a lot of stories. They're going through a lot of heavy stuff, and they have serious stories, but they also have funny stories. They have wonderful stories of "kiddom," of being who they are.

I'll give you a wonderful moment that was the first paper of the year last year. My first paper is always "What did you do last summer?" The kids go crazy. I mean, it's such a grammar school topic. But I talk about finding a story, something that you are telling your friends now. Something had happened to you that would make a great story. What are you telling your buddies? Those are great stories! So, tell me the story on paper. So the kids are working on it, and a girl came up to me and she said, "I don't think I'm doing this right." I said, "What?" She said, "Well, my friend took this summer school class, and she's writing about what courses she took and her future plans, what she's going to do in college. And I'm writing about this lifeguard I wanted to pick up." I said, "What?" She said, "Yeah, there was this really cute lifeguard, and I was at the beach with my girlfriend." And she launched into this funny—I mean you talk about storytelling—I mean I wish I had this on tape—such a funny exchange of "Is he looking at me? No. Is he looking at me now? Yes!" That kind of exchange. I told her that her story sounded much more interesting than her friend's.

What kids need to know is that their job as a storyteller is to find the gold in the story and make that gold come alive. You see, we all know what's going on there. We've all been there. I mean, I've been on that beach wondering if that girl was looking at me and wondering how I looked. We've all experienced that universal "love thing" that goes on. Often kids say, "Nothing ever happens to me." But stories like this, stories they can relate to their own experience, show them that they do have stories to tell.

Personal stories are wonderful. I tell one about going to the symphony, and it ends up being a complete disaster with my daughter throwing up in the car. It's a funny story, a goofy story, about my kids and this goofy night. It's also a story that everybody knows, because we've all dragged our kids places that they didn't want to go and it didn't work. And we've all experienced these really embarrassing moments like when a kid throws up at a very bad time. I can tell that story to all age groups, even kindergartners.

Q: Why are personal stories so important?

A: It's a validating process. They learn their words can really touch someone. It puts them in touch with their own lives, the good and the bad. It gives them a tool to deal with their lives.

Q: How did you use storytelling in teaching?

A: Every Monday morning I'd walk in and say, "Are there any stories?" I was always telling them anecdotes, so... there was never a feeling that we were wasting time, because they always understood the importance of story.

Q: One final question. What about the performance of stories?

A: Well, I'm reminded of a story here. I was taking a class in performance from an instructor who was quite tough—and also a genius. He had a particular way of yelling at you if you weren't doing a good job. I was on stage doing something, and it wasn't very good, and he yelled, "Lieberman, if you're not going to do something special up there, why don't you just write down the story and hand it to me?" A line to remember for storytellers!

Note: Cassettes of the following tellings are available from Syd Lieberman by writing to him (2522 Ashland, Evanston, IL 60201, 708/328-6281): *The Old Man and Other Stories; A Winner and Other Stories; Joseph the Tailor and Other Jewish Tales; The Johnstown Flood of 1889; The Telltale Heart and Other Terrifying Tales.*

CHAPTER 5

•••••••••••••••••••••••

Taming Stories for Telling:
How to Prepare a Story

First, catch your story. The really exciting thing is that they are all around—out there—just waiting to be caught ... this "common possession of humankind—part of the deep structure of the grammar of our world."

Edie Garvey

T
HERE ARE those who say we need to thank Anansi—you know, Anansi the spider, the great trickster folk-hero of African lore. Stories, you see, were not always free to fly about as they do today. Oh no, and were it not for that crafty spider, they might still be confined to the box.

They say that once all stories belonged to Nyame, the Sky God, and that he kept them to himself in a beautifully carved wooden box. Little Anansi had the audacity to ask for the stories. Against impossible odds, the clever spider used his wits to win the magnificent box from the Sky God. Yes, Anansi was clever, but he was not always wise. In his excitement he threw open the box, expecting to gaze upon his stories as if they were precious stones. But stories have never been known to hold still. Liberated from the confines of the gods, the stories flew from the box like butterflies and filled the sky with rainbow colors. The frantic spider caught as many as he could, which explains why so many stories are known to us even today as Anansi stories. But the rest? They got away and flew to every corner of the earth. Anansi liberated the stories. No longer the property of the gods, the stories belong to all of us now—to children and teachers and grandparents and poets—to all of us willing to reach out to them. The stories are all around us now, just waiting for someone to catch them, and tame them, and share them with others.

I used to refer to the process of taming stories as "rehearsing" stories or "preparing" stories for telling. I have discovered that it is better to approach the stories as if they had a life of their own. Some stories eventually will become very tame, like the sweet old family dog who allows toddlers to climb all over him and pull his ears. Other stories, though they may permit you to tell them, will remain more elusive, more mysterious, more like the cat who has such a strong will of her own. The process of taming is one of getting close to the story and inviting it to be close to you so that you may share it with others.

Children sometimes ask me, "How did you learn that whole story? How did you ever memorize all those words?" When listeners ask if I know a story by heart, I have to ask them to clarify. If they mean, "Did you use your heart as well as your brain when you got to know that story?" I say, "Yes, by all means." But if they want to know whether I have committed each word to memory, I answer in a way that often surprises them. The truth is simple; I haven't memorized the words. Many people assume that you learn a story the same way you learn spelling words and the multiplication tables—by rote memorization. In fact, very little rote memorization is required in the process of taming a story, and the little bit of memorization there may be occurs only after the teller and story have taken some time to get to know each other.

Early in the process, most tellers are concerned with the shape of a story, with its plot. As Aristotle pointed out, the plot is what provides the skeletal framework on which to hang all other elements of the story. Learning the sequence of events—what happens—is a logical place to begin. This can be accomplished in many ways. Some tellers like to make an outline, grouping incidents into the beginning (exposition), middle (complications, rising action, crisis), and end (resolution). Other tellers, thinking like film makers, create a storyboard in which a series of pictures illustrate the tale. Some tellers in this, the computer age, think of story structure in terms of flowcharts, mapping the development of story with arrows and boxes. Flowcharts, maps, outlines, storyboards—the methods may vary, but a common strategy is first to clarify the sequence of events. In her classic text, *The Way of the Storyteller*, Ruth Sawyer (1957) states eloquently:

> Stories must be acquired by contemplation, by bringing the imagination to work constantly, intelligently upon them. And finally by that power to blow the breath of life into them. And the method? That of learning incident by incident, or picture by picture. Never word by word. (p. 142)

Learning a story "picture by picture"

Learning a story "picture by picture" is an especially powerful technique for many tellers. An exercise I use early in storytelling class involves children's picture books. I distribute the wordless picture books (*Good Dog Carl* by Alexandra Day is a personal favorite) and invite my students to read the books out loud to each other. They are astonished at how easy it is to "read" these books even though there is no text. The pictures tell the story; the images serve as a powerful stimulus for language. Even very young children are able to "pretend read," telling the story with the assistance of the visual clues of the pictures.

When my students are taming a story for telling, I invite them to imagine they are award-winning book illustrators. "What are the significant moments you would choose to illustrate in your best-selling picture book version of this story?" I invite them to envision their illustrations fully with as much detail as their imaginations can muster. With these vivid pictures in their mind's eye, they tell the story as effortlessly as if they were flipping through an internal picture book.

Create a memory graphic

One strategy for learning a story picture by picture is to create a *memory graphic,* or a graphic representation of the story. In my storytelling class, students make these as handouts for each other each time they share a new story. The handouts are free-form, but we've agreed to provide each other with the following information:

- bibliographic details
- plot synopsis
- story opening
- memory graphic
- characteristic phrases
- story closure

The *bibliographic details* and *plot synopsis* are straightforward, as you can see from the following examples. I urge tellers to include the story's first and last lines, or the *story opening* and *closing*, to help them begin and end each telling with grace and confidence. *Characteristic phrases* include repeated refrains ("Hundreds of cats, thousands of cats, millions and billions and trillions of cats!") or special language that will give a story its flavor. Story openings and closures are crafted in writing to help the teller begin and end with grace. But all of these components involve words, words, words.... It is the memory graphic that proves to be most helpful, as it steers us away from words and guides us into a realm of images.

The instructions I give are simple: tellers are asked to create a pictorial, graphic representation of the tale. That is, draw the story. Find a way on your handout to represent the story without using many words. Make a picture that helps you see the story unfold. Each memory graphic is unique. Some look like flowcharts, others like storyboards. Stick figures are fine because this is not a test of drawing skills. Humor helps. What is essential is that the teller think of the story in terms of imagery. In this part of preparing a story, the learning is shifting from a left-brain to a right-brain process. Thinking in terms of the memory graphic instead of the words invites a shift:

Left Brain	*Right Brain*
from linear thinking	to imagistic thinking
from seeing the parts	to seeing the whole
from informational aspects of thought	to emotional nuances
from seeing distinctions	to seeing connections

The memory graphic is a road map of sorts, helping us see the story in its entirety. Story flow, important characters, emotional tone—all can be conveyed in the graphic. And the process of creating it helps us move away from the concept that preparing a story for telling is simply a process of "learning the words."

The examples below were created by the students in preparation for their tellings. If you don't understand their graphics, don't worry. What matters is that the tellers understood them as they used these images to help take the story inside themselves. (The graphics are also helpful for tellers who wish to return to a story after having not looked at the text for a long time.)

Example 1: Talk⋆

An Ashanti folktale

Synopsis. A country man is digging in his garden one day, and his yam speaks to him: "Leave me alone!" To the man's great surprise, much of his small farmyard begins to speak to him. As he runs for the village, he meets three other men who are skeptical about his tale until inanimate objects begin to talk to them, too. They get an audience with the village's chief, who treats them with near disgust and turns them away. As a punchline, no sooner does he turn the men away than his stool speaks!

First Line. Once, not far from the city of Accra on the Gulf of Guinea, a country man went out to his garden to dig up some yams to take to market.

Memory Graphic.

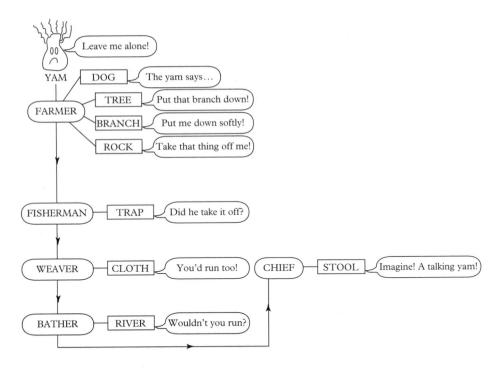

Characteristic Language. This story uses the device of repetition, as well as having talking characters that aren't supposed to be able to talk. It is fun to give the "talkers" characteristic voices, individual personalities. As for the repetition, the men (especially the farmer) tell their story along the road repeatedly, in increasing states of distress. You can speed up as you go along, and also gradually condense the actual text (especially quoting the "talkers") so that they are frenzied by the time they reach the chief.

Last Line. "Fantastic, isn't it?" his stool said. "Imagine, a talking yam!"

⋆ Prepared by storytelling student Lili-Anne Brown.

Example 2: The three sillies*

A traditional folktale from England

Synopsis. A gentleman, courting a farmer's daughter, dines with the family one evening and discovers that his hosts are three very silly people. They get hysterically upset over next to nothing and the gentleman vows to marry the daughter when he has found three people sillier than they. He comes across a woman who inadvertently hangs her cow and smothers herself, a man who doesn't know how to put on pants properly, and a village that believes the moon has fallen into a pond. Realizing that his three sillies at home are nothing in comparison to what he has seen, he returns home and marries the farmer's daughter.

First Line. Once upon a time there was a farmer and his wife who had one daughter, and she was courted by a gentleman.

Memory Graphic.

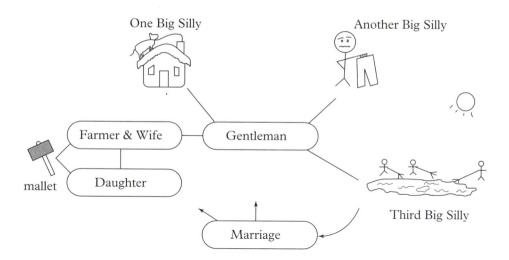

Characteristic Language. There are several repeated phrases and descriptive repetition in the first half of the story. Because the events of the gentleman's travels are so outlandish, they are a good opportunity for vocal and physical variation.

Last Line. So the gentleman turned back home again, and married the farmer's daughter, and if they don't live happily ever after, that's nothing to do with you or me.

* Prepared by storytelling student Tom Arvetis.

Example 3: The boy who drew cats*

Synopsis. A very small Japanese boy with great artistic talent for drawing cats is apprenticed to a village temple. He is asked to leave the temple due to his predilection for drawing cats in any empty space, and given some parting words of advice from the priest: "Avoid large places at night; keep to small." The boy journeys to a larger temple which is—unbeknownst to the boy— inhabited by a goblin-rat. The boy draws cats all over the temple walls before retiring for the night in a small cabinet (he has remembered, but not fully understood the priest's warning). His art comes to life to kill the goblin and make the boy a hero.

First Line. A long, long time ago in a small country village in Japan there lived a poor farmer and his wife.

Memory Graphic.

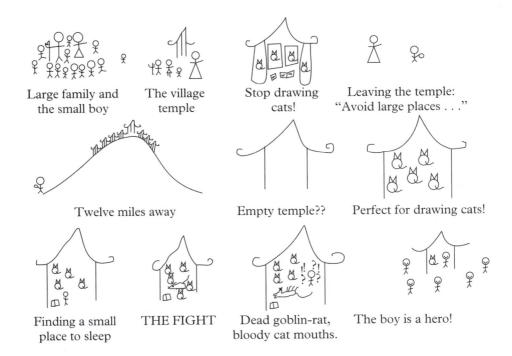

Large family and the small boy

The village temple

Stop drawing cats!

Leaving the temple: "Avoid large places . . ."

Twelve miles away

Empty temple??

Perfect for drawing cats!

Finding a small place to sleep

THE FIGHT

Dead goblin-rat, bloody cat mouths.

The boy is a hero!

---

* By Lafcadio Hearn from *75 Short Masterpieces: Stories from the World's Literature* edited by Roger B. Goodman, Bantam Books, 1961. Handout of "The Boy Who Drew Cats" was prepared by storytelling student Gillian Jorgensen.

Example 4: Millions of cats★

Synopsis. A very old woman and a very old man who live in a nice clean house are lonely. The very old woman wishes they owned a little cat. The very old man sets off to find a cat, traveling over hills and through valleys to find a hillside full of cats. He begins to choose one and continues to find another cat just as pretty, thus choosing them all and taking them home. Heading back, the cats become thirsty and drink a pond, each taking one sip; they get hungry and eat a hillside of grass, each taking one mouthful. Reaching home, the very old woman doesn't know what to do for she had only wanted one cat; so many cats will eat everything they have. The very old man didn't think of that and doesn't know what to do. The very old woman gets an idea to let the cats choose who should live with them. The very old man asks the cats who among them is the prettiest. Each cat says, "I am" and the cats begin to quarrel. The very old woman and very old man run inside their house until it grows quiet. They look out to see that the cats have eaten each other up. But in the tall grass, the very old man sees a little frightened kitten. They ask him how he avoided being eaten up. He tells them that he knew he was homely and didn't say anything when asked who was the prettiest; so they didn't bother with him. The very old man and very old woman take the cat in, give it a warm bath, brush its fur until it's shiny and soft, and feed the cat milk daily until it's nice and plump. The very old woman and the very old man decide that this is the most beautiful cat they have ever seen.

First Line. Once upon a time there was a very old man and a very old woman. They lived in a nice clean house which had flowers all around it, except where the door was. But they couldn't be happy because they were very lonely...

Memory Graphic.

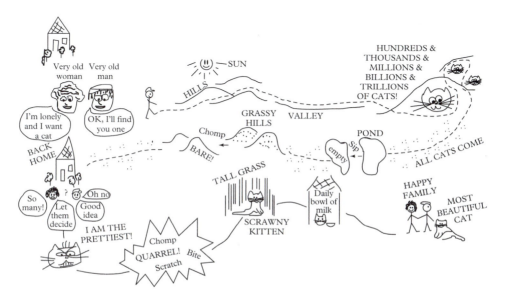

★ By Wanda Ga'g. Published by Coward-McCann, Inc., New York, 1928. Handout of *Millions of Cats* was prepared by storytelling student Angelique Gagnon.

Characteristic Language.

> "Cats here, cats there,
> Cats and kittens everywhere,
> Hundreds of cats,
> Thousands of cats,
> Millions and billions and trillions of cats."

And many references to "… hundreds and thousands and millions and billions and trillions of cats."

Last Line.

> "It is the most beautiful cat in the
> whole world," said the very old man.
> "I ought to know, for I've seen
> Hundreds of cats,
> Thousands of cats,
> Millions and billions and trillions of cats—
> and not one was as pretty as this one."

Conveying the story world and its people

Master storyteller Jay O'Callahan (1985) suggests the importance of tellers giving their stories a sense of place, using all of the senses to imagine the world of their story—its sights and smells, the specific sounds and textures and flavors that make this environment unique and alive. As a teller, you will want to convince your listeners that you have been to the world of the story and have returned to share it with them. If your story comes from a book with illustrations, you should pay special attention to the work of the artist. Often, rich details of the story are embedded in the illustrations; good tellers know how to mine the pictures for the gold they contain.

Just as you will wish to convince listeners that you actually have been to the world of the story ("You should have seen the way the tip of the beanstalk poked right through that cloud!"), so, too, will you wish to convey that you are well acquainted with the characters who people the story. Even if they lived long ago and far away, you speak of them from personal knowledge. To do this, you must spend some time fleshing out the characters. Work to understand their point of view. Imagine their appearance. Know what they want most in all the world. Experiment with their rhythms, posture, gestures, voices. When possible, make choices that will make your characters specific rather than general; it is always more interesting to encounter a person than a type. And the better acquainted you are with the people in your story, the richer your listeners' experience of them will be.

The role of memorization

At this point, some rote learning may be helpful. Repeated refrains are best memorized ("Little Pig, Little Pig, let me come in! Not by the hair of my chinny chin chin!"). So are riddles and proverbs. (Don't you think "A stitch in time saves a whole bunch" loses something in the paraphrasing?) Most tellers choose to memorize certain key phrases that give the language of the story its characteristic flavor. The popular folktale "Ol' Dry Fry" is given its Appalachian flavor by phrases like, "Law me! Hit's ol' Dry Fry! An' I believe we done kilt him. We got to get shed of the body quick or we're gonna be hung for murder!" "Gettin' shed of the body" is the kind of characteristic phrase worth memorizing; special language that brings life and flavor to the story is worth learning.

When it comes to rote learning, Garrison Keillor (1988) of *Prairie Home Companion* fame gives a very good piece of advice. He claims that the smartest thing he ever did as a storyteller was to memorize his beginning and ending "framing phrases." All of us who listened knew that when he told us it had been a quiet week in Lake Wobegone, the real story was about to begin. Strong women, good-looking men, and above-average children gave his stories closure. He said he took great comfort in these memorized lines; at least he always knew just how his stories were going to begin and end. Keillor knows that story openings and closings are vital to the success of a good telling. "Once upon a time, long, long, ago... at least three weeks before any of you were born..." is the sort of opening that can help listeners and teller enter the world of the story. Learning a phrase like Augusta Baker's (1977), "And so they lived, as why should they not, happily ever after," will help you give gracious and concise closure to your tellings.

Part of the genius of Lynn Rubright's (1994) storytelling seminars is that she offers her students opportunities to work out loud early in the process of taming stories for telling. The part of the brain that imagines the story and thinks of words to say is not the same part of the brain that actually produces speech. Anyone who has worked with stroke victims can verify this. How many actors, frustrated at a rehearsal when they can't remember their lines, swear vehemently, "But I knew these lines in my head." Although the process of working inside the head is useful, there comes a time when the storyteller simply must work out loud.

Practicing a storytelling

When the bare bones of story are clear, it is important to move away from the text and try a rough telling. Don't be discouraged if the early oral work is, well, awkward, to say the least. Winifred Ward (1952) wrote that the first tellings were often like "stirring up the muck at the bottom of the pond." After working out loud, the teller can go back to the text, see what was left out, and then return to the process of working orally. It is often helpful to tell the story to a partner who can support you with questions: Tell me more about this place. What time of year did this occur? What was the hag wearing? How did the old man feel at this point? Why didn't they just use their key? A partner's questions can help you clarify the murky parts, trim away what you don't need, and add specific details and feelings that will make the story richer. Jay O'Callahan (1985) notes that many of his stories were created with his children and family as early listeners.

If you can find a human being patient enough to work through your early tellings, treasure her; one of the most common hungers among tellers is to find a buddy who will listen and give loving criticism. In the absence of human beings, other opportunities are available to work out loud. Taking the dogs for a long walk is a great time to try on a telling. Showers and tubs are not only great for arias but they are also perfect rehearsal halls for tellers. They are relaxed places to play with your voice and the sounds you can make.

At this phase of the process, tellers are free to play with sounds and rhythm and language. Characters become clearer to you as you give voice to them. I have found dirty dishes, garden weeds, and the lawn mower to be excellent rehearsal partners, and here I find myself in the ancient family of all those who have used story to make the chores go by. I like to play with stories while I'm in the car (most storytellers have had some rather odd glances cast their way at stoplights). And though the automobile may offer a private space in which to work out loud, I should add a word of caution. Once, to my great surprise, I discovered I was in Indiana, not Illinois. It's a good idea to leave enough of your left brain behind the wheel to get you where you're going safely.

Another productive time to play with story is when you are falling asleep at night. Conjure images from your story as you fall asleep. Not only does this help plant the story deep within you but many tellers say they also have wonderful dreams about their stories. Let your mind wander through your story in that fertile morning dream time when you are neither awake nor asleep. By allowing for this time, you are inviting your innermost self, the wisest and most creative part of you, to work with you as you come together with story. Nothing works for everybody, but this may be useful for you.

This chapter has outlined several strategies:

- Learn the plot first.
- Make use of imaging.
- Flesh out the setting and characters.
- Memorize only a few select phrases.
- Play with the story out loud.
- Allow your inner self to be part of the process.

I encourage you, however, to approach these strategies with a healthy irreverence. They are not a recipe for learning stories. Stories and storytellers are far too varied to be encapsulated in anything rigid; each teller and story must find her own way to get to know each other.

Conclusion

Anansi freed the stories. They are there for all of us, but they are not tame. In *The Little Prince*, the boy encounters a fox and says, "Play with me."

> I cannot play with you," the fox said. "I am not tamed...."
> "What does that mean 'tame'?..."
> "It is an act too often neglected," said the fox. "It means to establish ties."
> "'To establish ties'?"

"Just that," said the fox. "To me, you are still nothing more than a little boy who is just like a hundred thousand other little boys. And I have no need of you. And you, on your part, have no need of me. To you, I am nothing more than a fox like a hundred thousand other foxes. But if you tame me, then we shall need each other. To me, you will be unique in all the world. To you, I shall be unique in all the world …"

"I am beginning to understand," said the little prince. "There is a flower … I think that she has tamed me …"

The fox gazed at the little prince for a long time.

"Please—tame me!" he said.

"I want to, very much," the little prince replied. "But I have not much time. I have friends to discover, and a great many things to understand."

"One only understands the things that one tames," said the fox. "Men have no more time to understand anything. They buy things all ready made at the shops. But there is no shop anywhere where one can buy friendship, and so men have no friends any more. If you want a friend, tame me …"

Perhaps there is a story, ancient or new, waiting for you to make ties, inviting you to become unique to each other. To share the story with others, you must spend time with it first. Perhaps there is a story, still slightly wild, whose eyes are trying to say, "If you please … tame me."

SUGGESTED READINGS & VIDEOS

Barton, Bob. 1986. *Tell Me Another.* Markham, Ontario: Pembroke.
Especially helpful is the chapter on "Making the Story Your Own."

Hamilton, Martha and Weiss, Mitch. 1990. *Children Tell Stories.* New York: Richard C. Owen.
Lucid advice for and from children. Appropriate for adults, too.

Livo, Norma J. and Rietz, Sandra. 1986. *Storytelling Process and Practice.* Littleton, CO: Libraries Unlimited.
This book includes excellent chapters on story mapping and planning and arranging storytelling events.

MacDonald, Margaret Read. 1993. *The Storytellers Start-Up Book.* Little Rock, AR: August House.
Great chapter entitled "Learning the Story in One Hour."

McGuire, Jack. 1985. *Creative Storytelling.* New York: McGraw-Hill.
One of the most interesting chapters in this text explains how to create your own stories for telling.

O'Callahan, Jay. 1985. *Master Class in Storytelling.* Marshfield, MA: Vineyard Productions.
In this video interview, an experienced teller shares his craft.

Rubright, Lynn. 1984. *Storytelling Teaching Tape.* Jonesborough, TN: NAPPS.
Offers step-by-step suggestions for learning and sharing a folktale, with additional activities to extend the learning.

Meet the storyteller...

Donna Washington

*Donna Washington is a professional storyteller
and actress.*

Photo by Tom Feezey

Q: We're trying to understand a day in the life
of a professional storyteller. You just returned
from a residency. Can you tell us what you did?

A: The school wanted stories about self-esteem.
I prepared ten to twelve stories. When I met with
the students, I asked them what kind of stories
they liked, and then I was able to construct my
package as I went along.

Q: What kind of stories did they like?

A: These children were in grades three through six. They liked ghost stories
and mysteries, and all types of adventure stories. So I told an Anansi story
about a very small spider who obtains the Sky God's stories from much larger creatures. I also told "The Wise King, the Cook and the Farmer" and did
creative drama with the students. In the middle of the story, the kids get to
decide what happens, so we stopped and restructured the story using their
ideas. Then I told the story of a wise queen, because I had just told the story
of a wise king! And we talked about how queens could be wise and brave just
like kings. Finally I told a very long story, "Wiley and the Hairy Man." I did
two sessions, each one an hour long.

Q: How did you become a professional storyteller?

A: I have always been interested in storytelling. There were always lots of
stories in my family. After dinner we'd sit around the table and my father
would tell stories. It was years before I realized my father had not lived six or
seven hundred years! He always told the stories in first person, so I thought
he had been there! In my junior year in college, I ran into professors who
were interested in storytelling—who taught storytelling and told stories. I
"hooked up" with these. My last year in college, I did showcases, told stories
in area schools, and had brochures printed, so when I graduated, I had
already made some connections and had some publicity ready to go.

Q: What kind of stories do you tell?

A: I tell international folk and fairytales—tales that show a person overcom-
ing something. I also like stories that show that when you are unkind to the
world around you, it will be unkind to you.

Q: Many of the tales you tell are African and African-American. Why do
you believe there is a need for such stories?

A: The African and African-American culture is rich in story. Brer Rabbit has recently been banned. That's horrible—the biggest African-American folk hero! That's a crime. Because he's quick and clever, he always escapes. That's a very big part of the African-American experience in the South. Brer Rabbit is African. The African-Americans took him and changed him into an African-American folk hero. Add eight hundred years, and someone decides he's derogatory. I find that impossible to believe.

Q: What do children like about the stories you tell?

A: Children love the magic. I tell a story, "The People Could Fly." I love that story—the images and the magic. How wonderful that there was a people who could fly! Every child's dream! The magic is so much a part of the African-American tradition because it was so needed. If you don't have anything, you come up with your own magic. Children love magic. I tell "Wiley and the Hairy Man" in obvious black dialect. But children aren't worried about whether Wiley is white or black or fuchsia. They're worried because he's a little boy stuck in a tree and the hairy man's coming. The dialect is black southern, and they don't care.

Q: Do you care?

A: Yes, I care. I care that they hear that. What they are hearing is cross-racial. Even though the dialect is not their own, the point of the story is the same for all children. I have a dedication to helping children to see the power of themselves. And to help African-American children see the power of being African-American and very beautiful.

Q: You're a trained actress. Do you see a difference in the two art forms of storytelling and acting?

A: Oh, yes, there's a difference. In storytelling you're given more power. You have to make the light, the sound, the action, all the characters. In theatre you have to be focused on your niche in the story. As a storyteller, I'm not a piece of the story. I am the story.

Note: Donna Washington's stories are featured on the African-American tape of the multiethnic Heritage Series, published by Children's Press, 5440 North Cumberland, Chicago, IL 60656.

CHAPTER 6

•••••••••••••••••••••

The Story Is in the Telling:
Finding Your Own Voice

Storytelling is a kind of music with the storyteller as the instrument.

Jay O'Callahan

I 'VE HEARD tell that a long time ago when the world was very, very young, the creature we now know as Frog was very unhappy. "No tail," he wailed, "No tail at all!" He went before Nyame, the great and powerful Sky God, and demanded justice. "Lion has a tail. Tiger has a tail. Elephant, Monkey, Hedgehog … why even Lizard has a tail! They all make fun of me. Please, Sky God, send me a tail of my own." After a silence, Nyame spoke. "With your tail will come a task. Will you tend to my well and share its sweet water with all who are thirsty?" "Of course I will," croaked Frog eagerly. In return for that promise, the Sky God sent him a most beautiful tail, unlike any we see in these parts today.

For a time, all was well—until the rains refused to fall and a terrible drought came upon the land. One by one the streams and rivers dried up. When the parched animals came to the well, Frog turned them away, saying, "There's no water here." Creatures large and small were denied. Smelling a broken promise, Nyame came to investigate. Without looking to see who it was, Frog called out, "There's no water here!" Furious, Nyame made Frog's tail wither and disappear. To keep Frog from forgetting, new frogs are born with tails they lose as they grow up. So it is to this very day, helping us all to remember that which Frog discovered long ago: A good "tale" is meant to be shared!

Stories are meant to be told. After all, look what happened to Frog. This chapter offers practical advice about the art of sharing stories with listeners. But first, a word of caution. Do not look here for the single right way to tell stories. There is simply no such thing. There are as many right ways to tell stories as there are stories to tell. That may be the single most important sentence for you in this book, so I'll say it again. *There are as many right ways to tell stories as there are stories to tell.* The art is in discovering which way is most appropriate for you.

The best teachers are not those who teach what to say or even how to say it. Brilliant teachers of storytelling, such as Donald Doyle and Lynn Rubright, don't subscribe to a single school of storytelling; they coach each teller individually, helping each to discover her own beauty and power. They help each teller find her own voice and give her the confidence to tell in her own way, unique in all the world. The teachers who transform are those who help students discover their own voices and give them the confidence to speak for themselves.

What kind of a storyteller are you?

When I think of all the successful tellers I know, I am astonished by the diversity of the many styles of telling. Some tellers make you feel as if you are rocking on a back porch on a lazy summer afternoon. Other storytellers seem more like actors, performing stories in a theatrical fashion. Still other tellers create an aura of spiritual mystery, telling in the formal, ritualized manner appropriate for the world's sacred stories.

Is one way of telling stories better than another? Not in my opinion. Many potential tellers are afraid to try storytelling, saying, "But I could never tell like she does." It took me a while to discover that nobody expects you to tell like anybody else. The secret is to find the way that's right for you. A series of descriptive adjectives, arranged as polar pairs, may help clarify the diversity of successful ways to tell stories. These are intended to be descriptive, not prescriptive. They do not presume to judge any specific style of storytelling, merely to help us see that learning to tell stories is the kind of problem that has multiple correct solutions.

Continuum 1: Dramatic quality

CONVERSATIONAL ◆ ———————————————— ◆ THEATRICAL

Should tellers be conversational or theatrical? Great debates are waged concerning this one, and the arguments are not terribly useful. Donald Doyle, an actor by training, brings the riches of the theater with him to his storytelling. He has a trained, resonant voice and has the dialects of world speech at his command. He creates vivid characters, experiences moments in their emotional fullness, and tells with a sensitivity to the rhythms of language and the power of silence. Jay O'Callahan and Lynn Rubright are also quite theatrical in their styles of telling.

At the conversational side of the continuum is a wonderful storyteller, Betty Weeks, a brilliant kindergarten teacher who "retired" in 1991. (See "Meet the Storyteller... at the end of this chapter.) She tells in a rapid-fire style, which also happens to be the way she talks. Using almost no gestures, making little effort to vary the pitch of her voice, and not indicating change of characters, she is as far from the theatrical end of the continuum as you can imagine. And her tellings are adored. Without the trappings of performance, the teller becomes invisible and the story becomes most important. Young children and adults listen intently as the story lives in their imaginations.

Betty is well known in the Chicago area for her workshops. She tells of the time she shared a program for teachers with a highly theatrical teller: "... beautiful, long black hair, a graceful, dancer's body, and a very dramatic voice ... and here I was, a kindergarten teacher with gray hair. I was scared to death." After the program she was surrounded by teachers shaking her hand. "Thank you so much," they all said to me. "After watching that first teller, we were sure we could never do storytelling. But now that we've seen you tell, we're convinced that almost anybody can do it." Betty relates this story with a twinkle in her eye, but there is wisdom in the reassurance of her conversational style of telling.

Few people set out to be storytellers at the beginning of their professional lives. Storytelling tends to be a "back door" art form that people discover after they have been seriously pursuing something else. That "something else" usually influences where storytellers find themselves on the continuum. With notable exceptions, those who come to storytelling from the worlds of education, children's literature, and library science tend to find themselves closer to the conversational end of the continuum. Those who come from the performing arts often find themselves closer to the theatrical end. There is room for tellers at all points of the continuum. And all have something to learn from each other.

Continuum 2: Point of view

THIRD PERSON ◆ ——————————————————— ◆ FIRST PERSON

Some tellers tell about the story, and others tell from within it, stepping into character as they speak. One teller may explain that, "The wolf beat his fist upon the door and demanded in no uncertain terms to be permitted entrance," and another teller may curl her lip and growl, "Little Pig, Little Pig, let me come in!" Neither way is more inherently correct, but one may feel better for you and your listeners.

Most tellers strive to move fluidly from the perspective of narrator to that of character and back again. To keep this movement fluid, characters usually are suggested rather than fully developed. I work to assume the attitude and feelings of a character without radically shifting my voice and body. I don't use falsetto voices when I portray women; instead, I focus on the truth of the moment and work to suggest the spirit of the character as simply and honestly as I can.

Continuum 3: Commitment of story to memory

FULLY MEMORIZED ◆ ————————————— ◆ FULLY IMPROVISED

Memorization occurs in differing degrees for different tellers. Storyteller Syd Lieberman explains that his stories have become polished smooth like a stone he has been rubbing. Now they emerge consistently in each telling, the language remaining virtually unchanged. Through repeated tellings his stories have become memorized, and he is comfortable with them this way. Lynn Rubright, on the other hand, enjoys creating spontaneously with her listeners. She asks her listeners for ideas and is comfortable with long stretches of story that are completely improvised. Most tellers (the authors of this book included) use rote memorization sparingly, learning only characteristic phrases, repeated refrains, and strong beginnings and endings, leaving the rest of the story open to the variety that occurs with listeners in each specific telling.

Continuum 4: Vocal life

UNDERSTATED ◆ ——————————————————— ◆ ANIMATED

I will never forget riding in a taxi with Jay O'Callahan. While the cabbie and I chatted, Jay stared out the window at Lake Michigan, humming, blowing motor boat sounds through his lips, yawning loudly, and spewing nonsense syllables. The friendly cabbie (not an oxymoron in Chicago) was too kind to ask if I was escorting my friend to a home for the bewildered, but I can only imagine what he must have been thinking. Jay, of course, was preparing his voice for performance, and this warm-up ritual is necessary given the demands he places on his voice in each telling. Character voices, songs, varied rhythms, and expressive tone qualities are hallmarks of his work. Lynn Rubright, too, uses her voice with musical expressiveness; her stories often take on the qualities of folk operas.

Donald Davis tells a story called "The Crack of Dawn," which you can see on video in the American Storyteller Series. This is a brilliant, mesmerizing telling in which the storyteller shares memories of his great-aunt Laura. The style of telling is conversational and understated. One student remarked, "Why, he's just plain talking!" From the simplicity of his "plain talking" emerges a story of great beauty and power.

Continuum 5: Physicalization

STATIONARY ◆ ——————————————————— ◆ ACTIVE

Should I sit or should I stand? Should I use movement and gesture or should I hold still? Every teller wrestles with these questions, and there is a range of correct answers. Some tellers are extremely active as they tell. Lynn Rubright incorporates mime and dance into her tellings as she steps into each character. When she tells of ice skating, her arms swing at her sides; as she creates the giant Bally Sally Cato, she steps with huge strides. Our beloved Betty Weeks, in contrast, remains seated in her chair as she shares her folktales, often with her hands in her lap. Don Davis sits on a porch swing as he gently tells the story of his great-aunt Laura. Jackie Torrence, one of America's most loved storytellers, usually sits on a piano bench to tell her stories. She is a large woman who seems to be most at ease when she is seated. Without leaving the bench, she animates the stories with her beautiful hands, her expressive face, and her unforgettable eyes.

I have found that students new to the art form of storytelling take comfort in these polar pair adjectives. All of us are reassured to learn that there are many ways to tell stories, and that we can bring our unique loves and talents to the process. "May I sit in a chair and just 'plain talk' my story?" Yes. In fact, that is often the most powerful way to tell. "Would it be okay for me to strum my guitar and add a folksong to my story?" Of course. Storytellers have been singing for thousands of years. "Is it all right for me to step into character and act out part of my story?" By all means. Don Doyle and Jay O'Callahan do it all the time. "Yes, but is it all right if I don't tell like they do?" Of course. Be open to all the possibilities for storytellers, and strive to find the style that is most right for you.

What influences the way that you will tell the story?

Finding your own voice is an ongoing, dynamic process. Don't be surprised if your voice changes—from telling to telling, from story to story, from listener to listener. Each story will call you to tell it in a certain way. The stories that Anansi set free have a life of their own; if you are open to them, they will inform your style of telling. Each story will have its influence on your voice, calling you to tell in a certain way. My family stories, especially those about my young daughter, tend to be intimate and gentle; they call me to tell them in a simple, honest, conversational style. They feel best when I sit down to tell them and share them without elaborate gestures or movements. On the other hand, folktales such as "Wicked John and the Devil" and "Ol' Dry Fry" lend themselves to a broader, more theatrical style of telling. The whole body gets involved as Wicked John hammers the anvil, and the face of the woman discovering Ol' Dry Fry hanging upside down in the smokehouse is fully animated. In finding your own voice as a teller, it is wise to be open to the voice of the story to be shared.

Just as each story will influence your voice as a teller, so, too, will each room and each group of listeners. After performing a series of one-person shows, Broadway singer Mandy Patinkin described the art of "tuning the hall." Each space has its own peculiar acoustic qualities, and Patinkin spends time discovering the best sound possibilities in each space. Storytellers, too, must "tune the hall" as they gauge the appropriateness of their telling in each particular space. I was fortunate to observe Jay O'Callahan do this as he performed at a family gathering. The evening before, he had been performing in a large theater to more than five hundred people. The performance was stunning. He was able to project his voice without a microphone, and he used broad gestures, dancelike movement, and an animated face to reach every seat in the house. At the family gathering, his telling changed. The volume was "tuned" to be appropriate for a living room, not a theater. The movement was more spare (he did not knock over a single lamp), and he connected with those specific family members who had gathered to hear this story for the first time.

My daughter Caitlin also has taught me about tuning the hall. I learned (the hard way) that the style of telling I use to engage large groups of children in a gymnasium is not appropriate for bedtime—unless we all want to stay up past midnight. My daughter and I have a special story for bedtime now. It's all about a bunny named Philly and her mother, Sarah, and how they go to sleep after a day of hopping. The story probably won't stand on its literary merits, but we made it up together. Caitlin lies on her tummy, and the story is told in the dark with the characters hopping around gently on her back. My fingers trace the story gently between her shoulder blades, and my voice barely rises above a whisper as Philly and Sarah and Caitlin fall asleep in a bed of grass and leaves and flowers and clover. It's a time we both enjoy, but I had to learn that different occasions call for different styles of telling.

Some tellers perform in the classroom as if they were on a grand stage; others perform in a large space as if they were in an intimate story corner of the library. Neither is satisfying. The best tellers learn to "tune the hall," adapting their style to fit the specific needs of each telling.

There are as many right ways to tells stories as there are stories to tell. Find your own voice and respond to the variables of

> the space;
> the occasion;
> the listeners;
> the story; and, of course,
> you.

Ten tips for tales well told

The following suggestions apply to a variety of settings and styles. They are designed to support you in your tellings.

1. Enjoy rapport with listeners.

One of the unique characteristics of storytelling is the special rapport developed between the listeners and the teller. Unlike the theater, in which actors usually don't acknowledge the presence of the audience, storytellers speak directly to their listeners. Stand-up comedians acknowledge the audience, but they may be hostile to some or all of them if this will evoke laughter. Whereas the theater has an "invisible rapport" with the audience and the comedian has a potentially antagonistic relationship with the crowd, the storyteller has an open, benevolent relationship with the listeners as they come together for the shared experience of a story. The best storytellers approach their audiences with respect, avoiding preaching or condescension at every turn. A special bond is created when tellers share a story they love with listeners they care about.

Jane Yolen (1986) speaks of this rapport between listeners and tellers when she describes storytelling as "that which is private becoming public and that which is public becoming private." Lynn Rubright refers to storytelling poetically as an intimate art form that exists "eye to eye and heart to heart." Certainly, eye contact is one of the hallmarks of storytelling, whether it be with large groups or small. Beginning tellers often have difficulty making eye contact with their listeners, looking instead at the floor or the ceiling or at their hands. Unfortunately, this comes across as a lack of interest (or fear) and leaves the listeners feeling left out of the telling. Other beginning tellers think that making eye contact involves staring intently at a sea of listeners throughout the sharing of a story, and the result is a frozen, unsatisfying attempt at building rapport with listeners.

Borrowing from actor training, I have found it useful to discuss eye contact in terms of "circles of awareness." At the risk of adding new jargon, four "circles" (or "bubbles," when I am working with young children) can help the teller include others in the presentation of a story. Moving easily from circle to circle is the goal of good storytellers, as the sharing process is dynamic and fluid.

The First Circle. The first circle of awareness is a private one. It involves just you as teller—your feelings, memories, and imagined images. When a teller goes into the first circle, she goes into herself. As listeners, we are aware that she is experiencing something important and specific. When the teller is in first circle, she is not making direct eye contact with the listeners. At this moment, her eyes may even be closed for the memory of a specific image or feeling. The first circle of awareness does not include the audience, for the teller is, in essence, making eye contact with herself. When I see a teller use first circle effectively, I know the story is important to her. The teller becomes invested in the telling as she experiences its inner life.

The use of this circle is important but limited in the telling of stories. Obviously, an entire story told in first circle would leave the audience feeling left out. Too often in their eagerness to connect with listeners, however, tellers don't allow themselves even brief moments in first circle. Brief, private, first circle moments fuel the teller and add to the believability of the telling.

The Second Circle. The second circle of awareness also is offered in the presence of the listeners but does not include them directly. The second circle does include awareness of the place and characters in the story, but not of the audience. When I am in second circle, my eyes may focus on an imagined character or object in my story. For example, my eyes may look upward at those of an imaginary giant as I say, "Goliath, I have been sent by my people to fight you." Or my eyes may focus on the palm of my hand, where I am holding a pair of tiny magic shoes left to me by the fairies. If the teller vividly imagines these second circle moments, they will be real for the audience, too.

The Third and Fourth Circles. Both the third and the fourth circles of awareness take the audience directly into account. The third circle involves direct eye contact with one or two members of the audience, and the fourth encompasses the entire audience. When telling in fourth circle, I include the entire audience as if it were a single listener; when telling in third circle, I focus on a single listener as if she were the entire audience.

Movie images may help clarify third and fourth circles of awareness. Sometimes I imagine that my eyes are the lenses of a movie camera filming the audience. When I am in fourth circle, my eyes are filming the whole audience at once in a long shot or a sweeping pan. When I move to third circle, my eyes zoom in for a close-up of a small portion of the audience. I am careful not to stay zoomed-in on any one person for too long (nobody should feel picked upon), but I do make an effort to connect with everyone at some point in the telling. This constant flow from fourth to third circles, scanning and zooming if you like, allows me to make eye contact with specific individuals while including the whole audience.

These four circles are useful to describe the teller's focus and extent of audience inclusion, but of course they are used with more common sense and intuition than conscious technique. Some beginning tellers may have to be coached to venture into different circles; others find this occurs quite instinctively. For all of us who share stories, the goal is to move freely from circle to circle as we reexperience the story ourselves and share it with an audience.

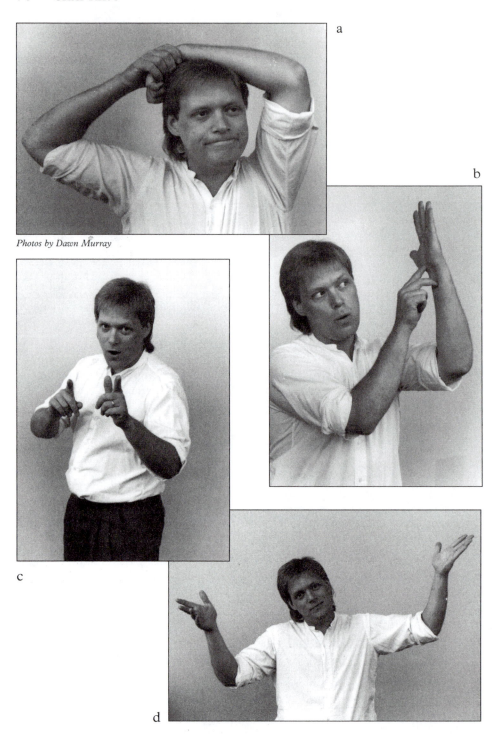

Photos by Dawn Murray

Circles of awareness: (a) The first circle—the storyteller sees an image in his mind's eye; (b) the second circle—eye focus in the world of story; (c) the third circle—eye contact with one audience member; and (d) the fourth circle—eyes take in the entire audience.

2. Create a sense of occasion.

Storytellers help us move from our everyday world into the world of story. One way to do this is to treat the act of coming together to share a story as something special. Like a birthday or holiday or rite of passage, the storytelling is given a sense of occasion. Kindergarten teacher Betty Weeks writes the day's activities on the board at the beginning of the morning. Two o'clock: Storytelling! There it is on the board in big letters for all to see and look forward to all day long. Rituals keep life's important moments from slipping away too quickly, and storytellers often use ritual to help us enter the world of story. Laurel Serleth gathers her students on a special rug for the sharing of stories. Nancy Donoval keeps a pouch filled with stories. She opens the pouch slowly, so as not to let all the stories fly out at once, and shares the story that most want to be told that day. Augusta Baker is legendary for a candle she lit at the beginning of story hour; everyone knew she was in the world of story until the candle was blown out, usually by a volunteer from her audience, at the end of the hour—which always passed too quickly.

Storytellers also give a sense of occasion by introducing their tellings. Although this can be done in many ways, the best always seem to communicate:

- This story is important to me as a teller.
- This story has been chosen for you.

In a college classroom a student introduced her telling by saying, "When I was in sixth grade, I loved this story so much that I did something awful. I ripped it out of our book. I still have it and, especially when life gets confusing, I still read it." We listeners couldn't wait to hear the story that was obviously so important to our teller. Another captivating introduction convinced us that the story was not only important to the teller but it had significance for us as well. The teller grinned slyly and said, "With Halloween just around the corner, I thought you'd better hear this story. With all the ghosts and witches about to arrive, I didn't want what happened to poor Ichabod to happen to you." In these examples the tellers were able to give the story a sense of occasion with their introductions.

3. Orchestrate the telling.

Celebrate sound. The voice is the instrument you play as you tell. Whether your style is conversational or dramatic, it is important to vary the sounds you create to sustain interest. Pitch, volume, rate, tone—all are variables that the teller controls. Varying these elements prevents the story from becoming predictable and allows you to create moods and express the feelings within the tale. Variety is the spice of speech.

Finding the best pitch for you is important. Tellers experiencing nervousness (who doesn't?) tend to speak too fast and too high. Sometimes, I whisper to myself, "low and slow," just before beginning. This helps me find a pleasing, relaxed tone.

Of course, the first requirement of good volume is that everyone must be able to hear you without straining to listen. If your voice is too soft, you will lose the interest of your listeners. Some tellers, however, fall into the trap of being too loud; a bombast of sound is a sure way to push your listeners away. The goal is to find a middle ground everyone can hear, from which you can get louder and softer as you word-paint your story. Varying volume can produce exciting results, as it creates emphasis, expresses feelings, and establishes mood. "The jump" is a technique tellers of ghost stories use; listeners are drawn in by a soft voice only to be startled by a sudden explosion of sound: "Who has my golden arm? (softly) Who has my golden arm? (even more softly) Who has my golden arm? (just a whisper) Who has my golden ... YOU'VE GOT IT!"

Timing, as they used to say in vaudeville, is everything. Often, beginning tellers are convinced that getting louder is the key to making stories come alive, but I am convinced that the secret to beautiful tellings lies in rhythms, not decibels. Speeding up can keep action exciting or funny; slowing down will give words and ideas special importance.

I like to use *paralanguage* when I tell. Paralanguage may be defined as the vocal effects we use to communicate meaning, and these effects are sure to add life to a story. The "grrrrowl" of the wolf, the "bong, bong, booooonnnnnggggg" of the church bell, the hiccups of the ("hic") drunken man, the low whistle of the wind, the "sssssssssss" of the snake—all of these add to the aural life of the telling. My favorite book about paralanguage can be found in the humor section of your local bookstore. Frederick R. Newman's (1980) *Mouthsounds* guides the reader to create everything from trumpeting elephants to sputtering jalopies. The irreverent author provides a semitechnical guide that encourages the reader to *play* with the voice and experience a full range of vocal possibilities.

As an infant, my son, Ethan, reminded me that we learn to make vowel sounds long before we master the complexity of consonants. Babies delight in long, musical vowels—eeeeee, euhhhhh, ahhhhh, yah-yah-yaaah—the wonderful sounds we make long before we form our first words. As adults, however, we confine ourselves to short, clipped vowels in everyday speech. One sure way to add vocal life to a piece is to invite the teller to liberate the vowels from the prison of pedestrian conversation. "Hello" may resonate through a haunted house when it becomes "helloooooooohh"; "why" becomes poignant when asked "whyyyyyyy?"; "please" can be funny when it becomes "puh-leeeeeze." Vowels, long and playful, add feeling and color to speech. The vendors who hawk their wares, calling through the stands of Wrigley Field, know all about vowels. So does baby Ethan.

Silence, of course, is one of the most powerful choices you can make. Pauses allow listeners to image with you and share the impact of the story. Silence creates tension and builds suspense. Take for example: "And there (pause) coming toward me through the mist were two (pause) dinosaurs!" Compare that to: "And there coming through the mist were two dinosaurs!" In general, pauses create emphasis by communicating, "Listen to whatever comes right after the pause because it is really (pause) important."

4. Let your body talk.

Whether you are an active teller or one who does not use a great deal of movement and gesture, your body has power in the telling of the story. The human face is eloquent in the creation of humor and the expression of feelings. Jay

O'Callahan calls storytelling the "theater of the face" and asserts that few art forms reveal the beauty of the human face as well as storytelling does. Hands, too, tell stories, and the spine can straighten and relax to create characters and express feelings. Therefore, you should find gestures and postures that support your style of telling. All movement communicates, so controlling what your body is saying is important. Work to eliminate all nervous or excessive movement (brushing back your hair, for example, or shuffling your feet). As a general rule, don't move unless you have a good reason to. Be selective as you make choices about the physical life of your story.

5. Imagine!

The tale teller must create vivid images for himself if he wants his listeners to see them, too. See your story as you tell it. Like the shaman of old, you are reexperiencing your story. Tell as if you were witness to an event; remember that you are recounting images, not words. Encourage your listeners to imagine with all five of their senses as you include smells and textures and flavors along with the sights and sounds of your story.

6. Be present.

Be with your audience in the here and now. Storytelling is not a recitation; unlike a videotape, the teller can slightly modify each telling for the occasion. Make this telling unique for this audience. Sometimes the sky will be as blue as the dress Jessica is wearing today. When the wind blows open the window with a loud "bump," explain that when Jack was hiding from the Giant, he was as scared as we just were. Laugh with this group of listeners. Don't be surprised if no two groups respond to a story in exactly the same way, and don't expect this group of listeners to react the way another group has responded before. Impart a sense of spontaneity to your telling. I don't know how to practice this, but I do know that, with experience, you can learn to be open to the magic of here-and-now telling.

7. Celebrate ethnicity.

Celebrate ethnicity with respect and love. One guaranteed way to improve a telling is to explore its ethnicity. Sometimes a student will say, "And my grandma was yelling at my uncle...." I interrupt to ask, "Was she yelling in English?" "No, Italian (or Yiddish or German or Spanish)." When I ask them to retell that part with phrases in the original language, the storytelling always becomes more vibrant and authentic. Ethnicity shared with love helps us see into the cultures of others and affirms the universal nature of human experience.

Telling stories from around the world helps us to perceive the nature of the human family. I often tell my students to find a folktale from their own ethnic heritage, a tale their ancestors might have enjoyed. The results have been delightful. We have enjoyed tales from Russia, Wales, Mexico, Turkey, Japan, Ghana, Poland—the list is long and varied. The students share these stories with special pride, and we are all richer for having heard them.

8. Begin and end with grace.

As teller, you usher listeners into the world of a story and bring them out again. Memorize your first and last lines, and offer them with confidence. They provide much of the magic of your telling as they transport us to and from the story. Many wonderful phrases have been crafted to open and close the ports to the worlds of story. "Once upon a time" is perhaps the best known, but there are many others. Some of my favorites include:

Once, long, long ago, at least three weeks before any of you were born ...

Once, long ago, before yesterdays, before used-to-bes, back in the days when wishing did some good ...

The way it was told to me is the way I'll tell it to you. It went something like this ...

Long ago, in the dream time ...

Beyond the seven seas and beyond the seven mountains there lived ...

In addition to these traditional favorites, my students are getting good at creating their own story openers:

In my family, people are still talking about Uncle Harry. They say he was never the same since he began dancing with the cows ...

If you have trouble sleeping at night, maybe you'd better stop listening to this story right now ...

This story? This is a "Honey, grab-a-glass-of-milk-and-I'll-tell-you-about-my-first-love" kind of story ...

In Cuba, we do things differently ...

My grandfather's hair was white, and he used to brush it straight back with a silver brush. I still have the brush ...

Offered with confidence and eye contact, these opening lines arrest the attention of the audience. Getting started is the hardest part for many tellers. These carefully planned beginnings introduce the story and the listeners to each other and start the process of building rapport. For a storyteller, it is wonderful to have your listeners with you, eager to hear the story, right from the start.

Bringing the story to graceful closure is satisfying for teller and listeners alike. It is said that Mozart, when he was just a little boy, discovered a way to make his father crazy. He would wait for his dad to be in bed; then he would sneak down to the piano. Mozart then would play scales as if practicing. Finally, he would play one last scale, deliberately leaving off the last note. Do, Re, Mi, Fa, So, La, Ti.... Mozart's poor father couldn't stand the lack of resolution. He would have to get out of bed, come down to the piano, and plunk the last note of the scale (Do) before he could go back to sleep.

Beginning tellers, though not as cruel as the young trickster Mozart, may, too, deny their listeners the resolution of a telling. Often glad to have made it through their tale, they may shrug a quick, "The End," or simply stop abruptly. More experienced tellers have learned the value of a carefully phrased closing. Usually this last line is delivered slowly and offered with a cadence that brings finality to the telling. Some of my favorite traditional closings are:

Snit, snap, snout. My tale's told out!

And so they lived, as may we all, happily ever after.

… and if I'm not mistaken, they're living there to this very day.

Now that's a true story. And if it's not, it should be!

If the story was beautiful, the beauty belongs to all of us; if it was bad, the fault is only mine who told it.

And that, my friends, is the story of (title).

For the morning is wiser than the evening.

9. Savor the moments.

No wonder people have believed storytellers to be magical; storytellers can control time with their words. With language, storytellers can take us from the present to the future to the past. Years can pass in a single phrase (Rapunzel grew to be very beautiful, and when she was 12 years old she had long, golden hair), as the storyteller is free to skip past those elements not important to this telling of the story. Learning to omit the irrelevant is one of the most significant talents of the teller.

The teller is also free to expand time. Important moments, which often pass too quickly in real life, can be drawn out in the telling of a story. These moments should never be rushed. Placing a ring on a finger, dropping a rose into a grave, discovering dinosaur bones, seeing the old woman remove her head to braid her hair—these are all moments to savor.

At a recent workshop Jay O'Callahan (1991) coached a student to experience a moment more fully. The student shared a family story about the important discovery of a halo-like ring of feathers inside a down pillow. Jay helped her slow down the telling. In the telling that followed, she told us that the feather halo would be proof enough for her that the person who had died would go to heaven. She told us of the love for the person; it really mattered that the halo be there. Very slowly, she reached into the pillow. Gently, she sorted through the down. Her eyes lit up as she felt the ring before she could see it. She told of her hope. Gently, she pulled the feathers out, scared to death she might break the ring. Tears were in her eyes as she lifted the imaginary feather halo from the pillow. The moment, only hinted at in the first telling, was now complete in its emotional resonance. Slowing it down, investing it with importance, allowed both the teller and the listeners to savor the moment.

10. Relax and enjoy.

Stage fright. Jitters. Butterflies. Just the words make some people cringe. Speaking in front of people is scary; for some people it's particularly frightening.

Most everyone experiences stage fright at some time or another, even the most experienced veterans. Not to worry, however, for as storytellers, we are in a uniquely strong position to wrestle with this concern.

Recast the part! For a time I thought of stage fright as something to be overcome. I'd be preparing to tell a story, all seemed to be going well, and then suddenly "stage fright" would arrive. She would appear like an uninvited guest, hooded and spooky. Like the disenfranchised fairy in "Sleeping Beauty," she arrived at the last moment to curse the proceedings. I was afraid of her presence—if I could have thrown her out, I would have. I thought of how much better things would be if only this uninvited guest would quit showing up at the most important moments.

However, I then realized that this figure had been present at the most important moments of my life. As I thought back on past successes, I realized that she was always there. Perhaps she had not come to curse the proceedings, but to bless them. In my imagination I drew back her hood and discovered a benevolent face with eyes filled with kindness. Stage fright brought with her some real gifts to bestow—heightened sensory awareness, increased energy, and a sense that the moments I was experiencing were important ones that required my full presence. I've stumbled upon this secret: neither she nor her gifts are to be dreaded. Instead, I look forward to her arrival. When I'm first aware of her presence, I throw my arms around her. "Welcome," I exclaim inwardly. "I'm so glad you could make it." Embracing stage fright, acknowledging her presence, and recognizing her ability to bless the proceedings has made me so much more comfortable with her. Perhaps this recasting may be helpful for you as well. That stranger "stage fright" that you thought was a villain—who knows, she may well be a friend waiting to offer you her gifts.

Reframe the event. "ACK!" cried a new teller. "Everyone will be looking at me." For many, this is the scariest part, feeling the gaze of the listeners upon us. To help this new teller understand, I invited her to watch me tell a story to junior high students. After the story I asked these high-energy, pre-pubescent, image-conscious adolescents just what they saw while I was telling. "The triceratops at the window!" one exclaimed. "The tough construction worker," said another. "The girl with a baseball bat," offered a third. "I saw the whole thing—like a movie," said a boy wearing high-tops. Not a single student mentioned seeing me. Not one. Their gaze was on me, *but they were seeing the story.*

The new teller felt so much better when she understood that although people would be looking in her direction, their real vision would be inside their imaginations. As storytellers, we become invisible, serving the story as we help others see it in their mind's eye. Listening to those junior high comments, the teller also saw the audience in a new way. She realized they were not adversaries but partners. Audiences who gather to hear a story are called to join us in the creative work—they become our partners as the stories are given life in each listener's imagination. They are not the acid-tongued critics who review Broadway plays; they are the co-creators of a story. Fear melts away when we take the focus off ourselves and think about giving the gift of story to partners eager to share in the work.

So enjoy the process of telling stories. Relax. Jay O'Callahan (1991) refers to this relaxed, energized state as the "living room" feeling, encouraging tellers to feel at home when they share stories. Give yourself and your listeners permission to experience the sheer joy of a good tale. Share the story with enthusiasm, as if presenting a gift. Stories are meant to be shared, you know.

SUGGESTED READINGS & VIDEOS

The American Storytelling Series. 1987. New York: H. W. Wilson.

Eight videos feature stories told by twenty different tellers.

Baker, Augusta, and Greene, Ellin. 1977. *Storytelling: Art and Technique.* New York: Bowker.

This is a classic, rich book with strategies based on the authors' decades of experience. Practical suggestions for creating story programs in libraries.

Barton, Bob. 1986. *Tell Me Another.* Markham, Ontario: Pembroke.

Rich with insights from Canada's premier authority on storytelling.

Lipman, Doug. 1995. *The Storytelling Coach.* Little Rock, AR: August House.

Articulates an effective process for working with a storyteller.

MacDonald, Margaret Read. 1993. *The Storyteller's Start-Up Book.* Little Rock, AR: August House.

A jewel of a resource! Exceptionally rich bibliographies; practical advice that only a master teller could give.

Maguire, Jack. 1985. *Creative Storytelling: Choosing, Inventing, and Sharing Tales for Children.* New York: McGraw-Hill.

Filled with useful suggestions from an experienced teller.

Newman, Frederick R. 1980. *Mouthsounds.* New York: Workman.

This hilarious and useful book tells how to whistle, pop, click, and honk your way to social success. Comes with a record.

Meet the storyteller...

Betty Weeks

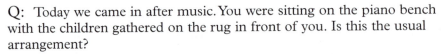

Betty Weeks retired in 1991 after twenty-five years of teaching—twenty-three of them at the Lab School of the National College of Education.

Photo by Sue Markson

Q: We just left your classroom in which we watched you telling stories. One you told was a new one for you, "The Foolish Frog." How do you decide what stories to tell?

A: I read that story over the weekend and decided to tell it. When I am looking for a story, I read until I find what I like, and I usually read ten to twelve stories before I find one I like. All of a sudden, something grabs me about a story and I know it's the story for me. "The Foolish Frog" caught me like that, and I knew I had to tell it.

Q: Today we came in after music. You were sitting on the piano bench with the children gathered on the rug in front of you. Is this the usual arrangement?

A: Yes, that's the story space. I need to see children's eyes, and I can't see their eyes if I'm sitting on the same level as they are. Their eyes tell me whether or not they are enjoying it, "getting" it—everything I need to know.

Q: How often do you tell stories to the children?

A: I tell at least once a day, and always at the end of the day because I want the children to leave school with the stories in their heads. If I tell at 10:30 A.M. and it's time for gym, well, there goes the story out of their heads. Whereas, if it's the last thing of the day, they often retell the story they've heard in class to their parents or baby brothers or sisters. So it definitely enhances oral language.

Q: What are other benefits to the child?

A: Children are making their own images, which they are deprived of because of our media-centered society. They are thinking and feeling—using both sides of their brain. They are getting their literary cultural inheritance. They are learning about other cultures and so, in a sense, stories bring the whole world together. They learn a sense of story structure, and they learn vocabulary in context. One thing I feel very strongly about is that in both what we read and what we tell, we need to use an elaborated vocabulary— enough so they all learn new words in context as they hear stories.

Q: The children in your class have heard the stories you tell several times. How do they respond to hearing stories again?

A: Oh, I think I tell every story ten, fifteen, twenty, maybe thirty times during the course of the year. On the child's birthday, the child gets to choose the story she has liked best during the year. In twenty-three years of teaching kindergarten, I have had only three children ask me to *read* the story. Most ask me to tell the story. They get something out of it every time. Just like when you read *War and Peace,* the more you read it, the more you take in. The same is true of listening to stories.

Q: How did you discover storytelling as a way to teach children?

A: I've been telling stories all my teaching career. I started my teaching career twenty-five years ago. I was a substitute teacher for two years because I still had a child at home. Well, you know how children treat substitutes! So if I saw the day was going to be difficult, I would ask the children to close their books and I would tell a story. Immediately I would hear, "Tell us another!" I would say, "I will—as soon as we get our work done." So I began to tell stories, and the more I told, the more powerful I knew storytelling was.

Q: Your delivery is very quick, very fast.

A: Well, I don't speed up just because I'm telling a story. This is the way I talk. So when I'm telling a story, I tell it the way I talk. But I have had children say, "Mrs. Weeks, you talk so fast your stories are too short." Or, "You talk so fast we have to listen fast." So I believe you must find your own way. And there are as many ways to tell stories as there are storytellers.

Q: Yet, there are so many teachers who are afraid to try storytelling.

A: I think what I do for teachers is to show them that all you have to do is to talk the story. Pick a good story and talk it. You don't have to worry about your voice or your acting ability or anything else. You don't memorize, so it's not a question of having to spend hours learning a story. It's fun.

Q: Do you ever invite the children to tell stories or do they retell stories?

A: They do retell stories, and they can do it verbatim. But they're also more free to tell their own stories because they've heard a lot of stories. I have a computer that is strictly a word processor. The children tell stories, we type it in, and then we print it and the children take the story home with them. So I definitely believe that storytelling encourages children to tell their own stories.

CHAPTER 7

• •

Bringing a Story to Life:
Story Dramatization with Listeners

As storytellers, we are not called upon to have the skill and talent to be believably someone else, as an actor is. What we are called upon to be is an authentic person ready to establish personal relationships with others and share our common heritage of stories of which the storyteller is the repository.

John Harrel

EVER SINCE Winifred Ward's seminal work at Northwestern University in the 1920s, storytelling and creative drama have enjoyed a kinship. Ward developed a method of telling stories and following them with a classroom drama activity. Creative drama is a powerful teaching tool that nurtures skills such as reading readiness, listening, self-expression, empathy, problem solving, and cooperation. As the teacher guides the students in improvised drama, everyone has the opportunity to make discoveries from within an experience. It is a joyful way to teach and learn.

Ward was an ardent lover of storytelling, and among her personal books now housed in the Northwestern archives are several storytelling texts, including a copy of Ruth Sawyer's (1977) *The Way of the Storyteller* with copious notes scrawled in the margins, and many anthologies of folktales and fairy stories. The legendary founder of creative dramatics was well versed in the art form of storytelling, and she worked to create a bridge between the two disciplines in the hybrid she called "story dramatization."

Story dramatization is a process that invites students of all ages to participate in acting out a story their teacher has shared with them. The teacher serves as storyteller and guide, first presenting a story, then harnessing students' natural propensities for make-believe in a dramatization of the story. Although the process is essentially the same for students of all grade levels, the material to be dramatized must be carefully selected for its age-appropriateness. The same process could be used to dramatize "Three Billy Goats Gruff" in elementary school, "Wiley and the Hairy Man" at the junior high level, and episodes from *Macbeth* in high school. I explain this process of bringing a story to life in the classroom to my university students by breaking it down into six steps, the six "P"s. At the risk of oversimplifying, the dramatization process is to:

1. Pique.
2. Present.
3. Plan.
4. Play.
5. Ponder.
6. Punctuate!

Pique

The first task of the teacher is to arouse the curiosity and pique the interest of the students. Master storyteller Donald Doyle calls this part of the process "baiting the hook," and when it is done well, students are eager to listen to a story before the teller has even begun. Ward suggested the use of a "motivator" to encourage this eager listening and offered many models of successful approaches. Props, photographs, discussion questions, rituals, games, songs—these are just a few of the strategies available to teachers to pique the interest of students.

The familiar fable of "The Tortoise and the Hare" will serve as an example for us to brainstorm effective motivators. I might begin this lesson by sharing a prop, a checkered flag, with my class and asking them what they know about it: who uses it and in what situation. Perhaps a student could even show me how it is used at the end of an exciting race. After just a few minutes of exploring the prop, I could begin my storytelling by saying, "I'm glad you know so much about races. They can be really thrilling, especially at the finish line. Let me tell you about one of the greatest races of all time."

This lesson might also begin with a photograph of a tortoise (or better still, a real one!) and a discussion in which we list, on the chalkboard, things we know about this creature: carries his house on his back; seems shy; eats leaves and bugs; lives a long time; moves very, very slowly.... This might comprise our list. From this, I could segue into the telling by saying, "Just when you think you know everything about someone, they turn around and surprise you. Let me tell you a story about a tortoise, maybe one just like this one, who surprised everybody."

The telling also could be introduced with a question for discussion: "What does it take to win a race?" After sharing ideas, I might say, "Let's see how you would answer that same question after I tell you this story about one of the most famous races of all time."

Another motivator might involve a game. A quick game of traditional tag is a sure way to energize a group, and "slow motion tag" (in which everyone moves and speaks in super slow motion) might help settle everyone down again. Or the leader might invite players to perform certain make-believe tasks (such as walking, playing basketball, cooking, exercising, conducting an orchestra, chasing a butterfly), at various speeds—normal, super slow, and oldtime-movie fast. From these games the story might begin, "We've played fast, and we've played slow! But I know a tale in which the two got mixed up. Fast was slow, and slow was fast. Listen, and I'll tell you just what happened."

Whatever the motivator, it should be brief, just enough to prime the pump. Beginning students sometimes create long, complicated introductions and find that they have made a tail that wags the dog. The function of the first "P" is to pique students' interest and prepare them for the telling to come.

Present

In the second "P" the teacher presents the story to be explored. The teacher is in the role of storyteller, and the students are in the role of imaginative listeners. For Winifred Ward, this presentation of the story was a valuable part of the drama process, and she insisted that telling the story was more valuable than reading it because of the special bond created between the students and the storyteller. The word "present" is used here as a verb; it is what the teller does. But we also may use this word as a noun, in which *present* becomes what the teller *gives*. The act of storytelling is much like offering a present, a gift, to those we care about. It is carefully wrapped in phrases such as, "Once upon a time," but we unwrap it together, slowly, as the story unfolds. Whether there is laughter or excitement or wisdom or suspense or healing inside, it is a present to be shared. The dual meaning of this second "P" reminds us that too often the emphasis in this presentational art form is on the act of performing rather than on the story as a gift to be offered. When the emphasis shifts to the joy of giving a present, anxiety about presenting often melts away. Ward encouraged this special classroom sharing between teacher and students as a particularly powerful use of storytelling.

Plan

The next phase in the process is a transitional one in which the students change from listeners to doers. Part of the excitement in this work comes from the opportunity to bring a story to life in the classroom. Students typically exclaim, "Not only did we hear a great story, but then we actually got to act out the good parts!" As much as they may have enjoyed the storytelling, for students anticipating the playing, the best is yet to come. Wise leaders channel this excitement by guiding the children to make some careful planning decisions before they put the story on its feet.

Ward often began with a brief discussion to allow the students to share their reactions to the story and reflect upon its content. Questions are usually the best place to start:

How does this story make you feel?

What did you like best about the story?

Will you tell me about the characters?

Did this story have any important ideas?

After this brief sharing, a series of decisions has to be made before a satisfying playing can begin.

1. *What part of the story shall we act out?*

Many leaders are most comfortable making this choice for the students. An entire story does not have to played. In fact, choosing an episode that lends itself to dramatization is often best. Even though the storyteller can take listeners anywhere in the mind's eye, the players are bound by the limitations of real space, real time, and their own skills and attitudes. The episode chosen must contain action that is appropriate and playable. Sometimes the leader can step in as storyteller and move the action in the voice of a narrator. Storytelling phrases such as these may provide the narrative link that will rescue leader and players from unplayable moments:

> *And so the wolf gobbled up the first little pig and then moved on to the next house. Then the prince kissed her gently on the lips, and when she awoke there were cheers of joy from everyone in the palace.*

These narrative links will rescue you from the potential violence of pig-gobbling and the embarrassment of princess-kissing, allowing the players to focus on the moments that benefit most from dramatization.

2. *Who are the characters who appear in this part of the story?*

Some teachers like to scribe for their students, writing character names on the board as the students offer them.

3. *What happens in this part of the story?*

Letting the students recap the action before the playing is helpful. Older students can handle longer, more complicated sequences of action. This recap should not provide a formal script but, instead, should serve as a guideline for what is to be acted out. Focusing on what happens, rather than on the exact wording of what is said, is best. Children will find their own words if they know what they want to accomplish.

4. *Now that we know what happens and who appears, what parts would you like to play?*

I have found it best to let students volunteer for roles rather than to assign them parts, although I sometimes will encourage a student to give a role a try. Because we are all pretending, and because we are trying to understand characters from the inside, everybody is free to explore every role. A boy may have the fun of playing the wicked witch; a girl may assert herself as the pirate captain. I insist only that they play the role sincerely, as believably as they can. The teacher should be open to opportunities for creative casting. In one playing of the "Three Billy Goats Gruff," we had a group of big, middle, and little goats confronting a family of grumpy trolls. In this way, everybody was able to participate.

5. *How shall we transform this space?*

Some dramas work just fine with everyone seated at the desk, but others suggest that we do some rearranging. Students have lots of ideas about this:

> Let's move the desks back to make lots of room.
> Let's use some chairs to make a bridge.
> Can the king sit at the teacher's desk?

Once we have reached consensus, I let the students do the work of adjusting the space to fit their drama. The drama will be more meaningful and more fun if it belongs to the players.

Play

At long last, the playing! The dramatization should have a clear beginning and ending point, and some signal that will stop the action. Many leaders use a drum or a tambourine to signal a stop; others blink the lights or call out "freeze" or "curtain." Sometimes these signal the end of a scene, but they also may allow the leader to add instructions and narrative links, or perhaps ask everyone to pause and think about what is happening in the drama.

Side-coaching is another leader strategy to be used during the playing. Side-coaching does not interrupt the flow of the play, as the teacher offers verbal suggestions during the action. ("And Mr. Hare got sleepier and sleepier. He started slowing down. Even slower. Oh, even slower than that, for even his ears and toes and tail were getting sleepy. Good! Do you think a little nap could possibly do any harm? Tell us what you're thinking, Mr. Hare, as you find a place to rest.") Side-coaching can be used to offer suggestions and encouragement, increasing individual commitment to the playing and making the drama more believable and exciting.

Ward encourages groups to play a scene more than once, and she cautions against being discouraged if the first attempts are "a little like stirring up the muck at the bottom of a pond." Each playing will improve as the participants grow in confidence—and they *will* grow in confidence!

Ponder

Experience without reflection is hollow. In pondering, the fifth "P" in the process, the leader's role is especially important. Although children naturally play make-believe, they are not likely to reflect upon their work without guidance. This phase calls for guided discussion of the playing. Here the students have the opportunity to articulate the discoveries they made from inside the story. They may talk about the feelings they experienced ("I felt angry when that little boy called 'wolf' to trick me a third time!" or, "I couldn't believe it! I was shocked when that tortoise crossed the finish line before me"). They also may make discoveries about the theme of the story ("Slow and steady tortoise kept going even when everybody was sure he would lose. He never gave up even though he was tired, too. A will to keep trying is part of being a winner"). Students also might learn about the quality and clarity of their expression during this phase ("I loved the way Mr. Hare got sleepy with his whole body. You could really see what he was feeling" or, "I had a good idea, but nobody seemed to hear it. Next time I'll say it even louder").

Obviously the way in which the leader phrases significant questions is essential to this phase of the learning process. Ward insisted that praise and encouragement come first, and it is powerful to see what happens to students when they know their work will be met with honest enthusiasm. Questions can be carefully phrased to elicit supportive comments from peers:

What did you like best about this playing?

When were the imaginations really at work?

When were the characters most believable?

What did you learn from the playing that we didn't know from the telling?

What did you learn about the important ideas in this story?

Constructive criticism also can be elicited in the questioning:

Did we leave out anything in this playing?

What would you like to try in our next playing of the scene?

What else could our characters do or say?

How can we make our playing even more believable?

After a period of pondering, more discoveries can be made as the story is played again. This loop of recasting, replaying, and evaluating can continue as long as the teacher likes.

Punctuate!

Bringing the experience to satisfying closure is an important part of the process. Donald Doyle calls this the "button" that lets everyone know the work is finished. There are many means to bring closure to a story dramatization. This activity frequently should be relaxing, to "cool down" an excited group before moving on to another activity. Rituals, songs, souvenirs, poetry—all may put a "button" on a story dramatization. For example, "The Tortoise and the Hare" could be brought to closure by presenting each child with a paper winner's ribbon, thanking her for her contribution to the drama. Sometimes a drum is passed around the circle, and each child is given the chance to beat the drum once and say what he liked best about the story and the drama.

The six steps—pique, present, plan, play, ponder, and punctuate—represent an approach for sharing stories and making dramas with your students. Here the storytelling is valued as an art form and then is used as a springboard for improvisation. Of course, this approach has infinite variations, and each teacher/teller will have to discover the way that works best with her students. This low-tech teaching strategy is so ancient as to be modern. The potential for significant learning is great as storytelling and creative drama come together in story dramatization.

SUGGESTED READINGS

Barton, Bob, and Booth, David. 1990. *Stories in the Classroom: Storytelling, Reading Aloud and Roleplaying with Children.* Portsmouth, NH: Heinemann.

This book deals powerfully with the use of story as a springboard for meaningful drama. It goes beyond traditional story dramatization and suggests multiple approaches to creating reflective dramas from stories.

Heinig, Ruth. 1992. *Improvisation with Favorite Tales*. Portsmouth, NH: Heinemann.

> *This user-friendly resource offers kid-tested strategies for bringing stories to life through drama. A wonderful book!*

McCaslin, Nellie. 1995. *Creative Drama in the Classroom*, 6th ed. New York: Longman.

> *Now in its 6th edition, this valuable work contains new resources connecting storytelling and creative drama.*

Ward, Winifred. 1952. *Stories to Dramatize*. New Orleans: Anchorage Press.

> *Still the definitive text on story dramatization, this book presents clear information on how to choose and dramatize stories. It also contains many stories, grouped by age-appropriateness.*

Meet the storyteller...

Ernie Love

Ernie Love, who has bachelor's degrees in political science and music education, as well as a master's degree in liberal studies from Northwestern University, teaches fourth grade at Crow Island School in Winnetka, Illinois.

Q: Yours is really a storytelling classroom.

A: It has evolved a lot, probably over the last four years. I don't come from a storytelling background. There was a lot of music going on in my house as I grew up; my mom dancing around the house, and all the musicals and classical and folk music—just all kinds. I'm sure my appreciation for music is from that time. But I don't remember ever being read to. I don't have stories. I don't remember them. So for me, this whole story thing began to develop when I became a teacher. I have no problem taking a chance in front of kids. I use lots of story starters. I was always telling stories and never finishing them. I'd been doing that for years and years. And I guess I didn't realize I was telling stories. So it's really in the last four years that I've become more conscious of—well, there being stories I really like and want to tell. I'm going to more festivals, and taking courses. I decided to get some training in storytelling to see what's coming naturally and see if I could get some coaching and some help. And it just became very much a part of me. I've done much more now over the last four years, as I've said, concentrating on oral language, which storytelling is part of. My writing program now is an extension of oral language. I spend much more time in the oral phase of work, even in the writing program work I'm doing with the children. So I see where the storytelling has also affected that.

Q: That's interesting. So you're saying that storytelling is affecting the writing that's happening in your classroom. Are there any other areas of your classroom that are being affected by storytelling?

A: Well, it fits in so naturally with community. Just in kids getting to know kids, in me getting to know kids, and kids getting to know me. It provides a good, safe buffer that allows me to talk about myself because you can frame it in story when it seems appropriate. One example that is coming to mind is when a child has an accident—falls, gets stitches, or whatever. It makes it very easy for me to talk about the memories of my stitches here and my stitches there. And to begin to frame it a little bit more as a story, not just, "Oh yeah, I got stitches too." But all of a sudden, with a story, you're saying, "You know, the doctor was standing right above me, and I can still feel his breath."

Q: Ernie, in your classroom—let me just see if I'm right about this—you tell stories, you model storytelling for your kids, and your kids tell stories.

A: Yeah, and it's structured very much as I mentioned before: the "stuff" of the curriculum is often taught through storytelling. I'll give you an example of what I mean by the "stuff" of curriculum. Geography: they're all sitting in pairs with maps on their desks of the United States, and I have them pass a pen back and forth. I say, "Why don't you put a border around the states that you have been in, where your feet have actually touched the ground." So the kids pass it back and forth. And I begin to facilitate conversations about them. "Tell what you were doing when you were there." This leads to some of their first travel stories. And then, "Pick one of those stories." And then, "Why don't you two sit down in this group of four and pick one of those stories and just tell everyone." So there they are in little storytelling circles around the room. Well, this can grow and eventually be one child telling his travel story to the whole group if he or she wants to. And that's just one example of how I stay with the oral language: I tell them, "You don't have to write it down. It's okay." And then at some point I may help them get into writing it down in an outline or cluster or mapping or picture: "Just make a picture or a series of pictures; anything you want that will serve as a memory of this experience." I'm considering that more and more in my thinking, whether it's theoretically right or wrong, I'm allowing myself to say, "All writing is an oral experience." I'm allowing myself to say that for right now as I work with kids because I get plenty of writing out of them, but now I'm allowing myself to say, "They're writing when they're just coming up with ideation. They're writing when they're just imaging and coming up with images." And that *is* writing and in fact the *writing* is after the fact. That's just another medium for the writing process; it's one of many. I'm allowing myself to do that more and more in my thinking in the classroom.

Q: Ernie, when I came to your classroom, I was aware of rituals that you have: things you do before somebody tells a story, things that you do after somebody tells a story. Can you tell us about those?

A: I have this set of logs that we nailed together that looks like your outdoor fire with orange and red paper coming out. We'll sit around this "fire" and tell stories. And I have something that a child will read every time to introduce the storytelling. It goes like this:

Long, long ago, people had no books to read.
Yet, there were always
stories to hear.
People told stories to their children,
and when their children grew up,
they told stories to their children, and so it went.
Long, long ago, people sat around the fire as night fell.
Their work was done and they rested.
The storyteller began a tale.
Everyone listened.

That's written on a little piece of paper that the children take turns reading. Everyone's sitting and it's read and that's our traditional way of saying, "It's starting, it's starting," and then everyone's ready. By the time it gets read, the kids have settled themselves and we're off into the story.

Q: And after the story?

A: After a child tells a story, the students get up as quietly as they can and take a blank paper and illustrate one vivid image that they remember from the story. They would do an illustration and then they would also write the story for that portion of the illustration. "Go ahead. You're the teller now. Don't describe the picture, but pretend you're telling. What would you say if you were the teller right now?" And then they give that to the teller. And I'd put it in an envelope for the storyteller and she gets to keep that in her portfolio.

Q: Can you tell us some other ways you use story?

A: A couple of years ago, a student, Greg, was a new student to the school and it was a rough start. He just was not accepted. Some of it he brought on himself, but he did not deserve what he was getting. He just didn't. It was one of those "new kid on the block" cases—they found something they could do to make it difficult for him, and they did it. Now as it happened, he was also a very open child with me. So, long story short, it got to the point where I said to him one day after school—and his mom was with him because we'd been talking about this. I said, "Do you trust me to try and make this better? I can't promise you it's going to be better, but can you trust me to try? Can I take a step?" And he just said, "Yes. Yes. Yes." So then, I planned a story. And the story that was perfect was "All Summer in a Day" by Ray Bradbury. So I read it the night before and I just put together in my mind a quick version of the telling and I told "All Summer in a Day," just under the guise of "Hey kids, I've got a story for you." I sat down, and I told it. And the response at the end was silence and the kids said, "That's kind of a strange story." I asked, "Why?"

"It doesn't have a happy ending."

I said, "Yeah, not so far. Maybe you could write something afterwards that could make it a happy ending." And I sat, looked around, and I saw a couple of heads down—the kids who, I think, were getting it. And I looked over and asked, "Is there someone in this classroom who we're treating harshly like the character in the story?" I just put it right out there, black and white. And the response came immediately from a couple kids. "Greg." And that started the whole thing. I have it on tape, and I'm just in awe as I watch the conversation get everything out and how all the energy shifts away from Greg to kids talking about all the times they were picked on. They just offered how this really wasn't fair. And by the time this had gone on—this was a long session, it went on for over an hour—I said, "I don't think you need me. The video's running, but I'm gonna leave." So, you know, I did let them know that I was spying. I said, "We're gonna look at this later, but I'm gonna leave, because I think this is a time you need to be with each other. So, you gotta pick someone to be in charge." And I just left. And Greg was in charge. That's on video. They picked Greg to be in charge. It happened, and it was magic.

Q: "All Summer in a Day" is the story about the persecution of a child by the group and the rejection of a child. And you gave that story to your kids and used it as a catalyst for them to work out the dynamics in their own room.

A: Storytelling becomes a safe medium. You put the story there and they have a chance to see themselves and each other in a new way. That's how the drama of storytelling can work.

Q: And you talked about the medicinal purposes of story. That was a healing story.

A: Oh yeah, and it did make a difference and we still had work to do, but it opened it up. We were looking at each other eye to eye. We knew the problem existed, so we could talk about it openly. And that provided at least a better way of communicating, and things did get better. That was a starting point; a very important place to start.

Q: Tell me a little bit about the way you've used storytelling to explore a whole novel.

A: Yeah, it was fun. *Sarah, Plain and Tall* was the novel. We read the novel and compared it to the movie—I like the idea of comparing two versions of the same story. Afterwards, I assigned the children to be experts of specific chapters as well as particular images from the movie. Then I prepared the kids for a storytelling event. We sat around our "fire" while I passed around bread and jelly and honey, and while we sat and ate, we told the entire novel from beginning to end. It took us over an hour. The chapter experts told when it was their turn or when they thought it was their turn, and we all just sat in silence, except for the tellers. I wish you could have seen the look on the children's faces when they realized that they had told the entire novel.

Q: Ernie, I think some teachers are intimidated by the process of learning a story or telling a story. What advice would you have for teachers?

A: First, don't feel that you have to memorize it. Second, it's not about performing. It's not a performance. Third, there is no one way to tell a story.

Q: You said it's not about performance. Do you ever tell kids, "This is a new one for me"?

A: Oh yeah. As a matter of fact, my kids provide a wonderful workshop atmosphere for me, and for them as well. Yes, I do workshops right in front of them for me. I'll say, "Now this is going to be your workshop, but I'm doing this for myself and you get to be a fly on the wall." I can tell one specific anecdote from last year's Hanuka time, and it just felt right for me. I knew about the story of Hirshel and the Hanuka Goblins, but I had not read it and I had not seen it. So I told them, before they were leaving for P.E., "Okay, I'm going to do a storytelling workshop on myself and you get to watch." And I went down to the library and I got the book and I said,

"I haven't opened it. Honest, I haven't. When you're at P.E., I'm going to read it and I'm going to put my memory aides on the blackboard." (I had worked with them on putting memory aides down on paper and ways that you can help yourself have visual memory.) So they went to P.E. and I read the story and I made some pictures, wrote some words down, and I wrote my memory aides on the board. They came back from P.E. and sat down and I just said, "Okay. I read the story while you were gone. And this is my first run-through. I haven't told it. I haven't practiced, but if I were at home, I might be talking to a teddy bear right now. I might be talking to a pillow. I might be talking out the window. I might even get Louise, my wife, to sit down and listen. But here goes." And I would just tell the story and I would say, "Oh, by the way, if you'll notice me looking over on the blackboard once in a while, it's because I'm doing what I would do at home if I had it written on paper: I might be carrying it in my hand. I might have it on the floor. I'd walk over to it once in a while as I'm telling, and I'd just look at it to help me go through it." I just told them, "That's my style of doing it the first time—go through it. Even though I know there are things that are going to be wrong, get through it." So I told the story. And then I reviewed for them, before they said anything, what I was aware of myself. Then I asked, "What things did I do that you thought worked well?" or "Did anything get in the way?" And they're great. They're wonderful critics. And it's such a safe place.

CHAPTER 8

•••••••••••••••••••••

Happily Ever After:
Exploring Storytelling
Through Activities

*I am also conscious that these stories, when told with a wealth of gesture
and expression of face and voice, are things of vivid beauty like rare
butterflies …*

C. G. Campbell

T HE ACTIVITIES in this chapter are those I have found to work. They
are in a somewhat chronological order, progressing from introductory
activities to critiquing activities. Although I have included a grade-level
suggestion for each, the level is somewhat arbitrary. Nearly all the activities can
be adapted for other grade levels. Although each activity has an objective, that
objective is not "written in stone"; the same activity could be used to meet a
number of objectives. For example, story mapping can be used to help students learn to visualize a story as well as to learn a story sequence. In short,
these are simply a group of activities that you can use as a starting point for
your own teaching and can be adapted as necessary to your specific students
and situation.

The underlying assumption for these activities is that the only way to learn
to tell stories is to tell them. Each person must find her own storytelling voice.
There are few rules or regulations. Whatever works for students is what they
should use. But, in any case, I am a firm believer in visualization. Students
should not memorize stories word for word. Rather, they should tell stories from
the visual images of those stories in their minds. As I tell my students: When you
tell an incident that happened to you, you don't memorize words; you tell the
incident from the images of that incident in your mind. Thus, the activities in this
chapter focus on telling from the visual image, not from memorization of words.

Many of the activities deal with the use of words, using language to create
an image in the listener's mind. In addition, many of the activities focus on
helping students use their bodies and voices to tell stories.

Finally, the emphasis in all the activities is fun. Storytelling is fun, and
thus, learning to tell stories should be fun.

• • • • • • • • • • • • • • • • • •

THE CAPTOR

Grade Level: 5–12
Objective: To define storytelling
Materials Needed: Leland Jacobs' "Storytelling, the Captor"
Procedure: Share the poem with your students. Ask them to define storytelling.

STORYTELLING, THE CAPTOR

Leland B. Jacobs

See the child, there —
Wrapped in attention
So alone in the midst of others,
Engrossed,
Held spellbound,
Oblivious to immediate time and place,
Caught by words,
The words of a storyteller.

What is this captor, storytelling?
Storytelling is communication between a possessor of a tale and a listener
  who wants to be possessed by the tale and the telling.

It is captivation:
The captivation of well-ordered plot,
Of lively characters,
Repetitive refrains,
Conversation,
Unfamiliar names,
Action and reaction;
The captivation of suspense,
Sympathy,
Laughter,
Of promise and fulfillment,
Disequilibrium and equilibrium,
Problem and solution,
Life's powerful forces at work.

It is relaxation:
Freedom from the immediate pressures of living,
Escape from the mundane,
Release from boredom,
Travail, tension;
The giving over the jurisdiction of
One's mind and heart
To impelling movement and sound,

To the enthrallment of word witchcraft;
The opening of the windows of being
To the fresh air of story art.

It is refreshment:
Feelings to savor,
Actions to view,
Thoughts to ponder,
Voices to hear,
Memories to cherish;

And enrichment:
New places to visit,
New people to know,
New stars to behold,
New hopes, new meanings,
New thresholds to cross.

It is involvement:
The tingle of fast-racing blood,
The tautness of nerve fibers,
The quickened beat of the heart,
The rhythmic movement of hands and feet,
The tilt of the head,
Goose pimples,
Eyes bright with wonder and delight,
Misty with sadness,
Mouth curled up at the corners,
Wide open in unrestrained mirth,
Fingers curling a lock of hair,
Thumb pressed against the lips,
Head nodding approval, or perhaps,
Emphatically saying, "no,"
Voice joining in refrain—
"Who goes trip-trap, trip-trap over my bridge,"
"Hundreds of cats, thousands of cats,"
"Acres and acres and acres of carrots,"
"Turn again, Whittington,
Thrice Lord Mayor of London."

It is kinship:
Kinship with Pooh,
Babar, Peter Churchmouse,
Mole, Toad, and Rat,
Georgie of Rabbit Hill,
Horton, Bambi, the Elephant's Child,
Misty of Chincoteague,
The Yearling;
Kinship with Twig,
The Saturdays, the Moffats,

Homer Price, Pippi Longstocking,
Henry Higgins, Mary Poppins,
And Janie Larkins with Blue Willow treasure;
With Sleeping Beauty,
Rumpelstiltskin,
The Wizard of Oz,
The Blue-Nosed Witch,
Pinocchio;
With Joseph and his coat of many colors,
And Esther, and Ruth,

And the Babe of Bethlehem;
Kinship with Pecos Bill,
Old Stormalong, Joe Magarac,
Anansi, William Tell,

And Ole Paul, the Mighty Logger;
Kinship with folks of other times—
Joe and Laurie,
Johnny Tremain,
Mary and Laura in the Little House in the Big Woods,
Huck Funn, Johnny Texas,
Caddie Woodlawn;
And other places—
Mei Li, Little Pear,
Kintu, Kanana, Kit and Kat.
Hans Brinker,
Long John Silver,
Shadrach,
And the Five Chinese Brothers.

And storytelling is more!
It is the electric circuit of the Familiar;
The highlighting of everyday adventure,
At home, at school, in the neighborhood,
With father and mother, brothers and sisters.
Friends, other children, other adults,

Like bakers and policemen, and gypsies and preachers;
With pets—dogs, cats, horses,
Rabbits and even bears and skunks;
The enlightenment of work-a-day experience,
The work and play, the light and shadow,
The tangibles of daily doings,
Bicycles and roller skates,
Dolls and precious toys,
Birthday cake, new shoes, and homes to take for granted,
The rainy day,
The bed-time ritual,
The church service,
The school play, and the picnic in the park;

The illumination of special times and happenings:
Birthdays and holidays,
The first day of school,
Unexpected guests,
New friends, new pets, new babies,
Secrets,
The day at the fair,
At the beach in the deep piney woods,
A visit to the grandparents',
A boat on the river,
A baseball game, a race, a contest won,

The lost, found,
The unpredictable, ordered,
The mystery solved,
The trial and tribulation past,
The sun of everyday, bright and sure and steadfast.

It is a bridge to the unfamiliar:
A passage to other places,
The great, grey, green, greasy Limpopo River,
Fog magic in Nova Scotia,
Shantytown, with a tree for Peter,
The Dakota prairies, blizzard-blown,
A holiday celebration on Olivero Street
A cabin in the mountains of Tennessee,
Wonderland,
The Golden Basket,
Mr. McGregor's Garden
Pancakes in Paris,
And Sherwood Forest.

An arch to interesting people:
Heidi at Grandmother's
Orville and Wilbur Wright at Kitty Hawk,
Crusoe and his man, Friday,
Pocahontas, Squanto, Sitting Bull,
Tante Odette,
Hetty and Hank, going "down, down the mountain,"
Shawneen, Angelo, Papa Small,
Mr. Popper, Dr. Doolittle, the Peterkins,
Henner's Lydia, Araminta, Chi-Wee,
George Washington Carver,
The Hojda, Miss Pickerell, the "Good Master,"
"And now, Miguel";

A span to other times:
A boy and a matchlock gun,
A boy with copper-toed boots,
Snow treasure in Norway,
Hidden treasure in Glaston,

Master Simon's well-kept garden,
Joel, Bob, and "The pulling bee,"
Abe who, to some folks, was "suthin' peculiarsom,"
Amos, mouse mentor to Ben Franklin,
David and Goliath,
Polly Patchwork, Little Owl Indian,
Mistrel Adam in abbey, inn, and manor house;
Tales of Nile or Nantucket,
Medieval castle or Indian camp,
Roman mystery,
Tales of rivers, prairies, and the rolling sea,
Tales of days long gone and deeds long done,
And once-familiar ways.

It is a gallery of memorable pictures:
Jim Hawkins in the apple barrel,
Ping on his Chinese Houseboat,
Little Toot busy on the river,
Mary, Colin, and Dikon in the secret garden,
The Little Red Lighthouse and the Great Gray Bridge,
Brer Rabbit, Brer Fox, and "dat brier patch,"
The Emperor, the child, and the crafty weavers,
Wanda Petronski's hundred dresses,
Bartholomew Cubbins' five hundred hats,
The Little House engulfed by the city,
Curious George on a bicycle,
And the night before Christmas.

This is the captor, storytelling.

See the child, there—
Absorbed, entranced,
Engulfed.
Ask him if it is not so.
But wait until the last story word is spoken,
Until, of his own volition, he breaks the spell,
Puts the period, says to himself, "The End."
Let him land and take off his wings.
He's been away a little while,
A voluntary captive of one
Who is a weaver with words.

Storytelling is a bond, an invisible agreement, a transaction of great worth
   between a weaver with words and one who treasures the weaving.

From Leland B. Jacobs, in *Creative Writing and Storytelling in Today's Schools*, edited by Paul Witty. Copyright © 1957 by National Council of Teachers of English, Urbana, IL. Used by permission.

WE ALL HAVE SONGS

Grade Level: 5–12

Objectives: To introduce storytelling and to understand that all of us have stories to tell

Materials Needed: A copy of "We All Have Songs" for each student and magazines to create a photo collage

Procedure: Have the class read the lyrics of the song together. Discuss the author's ideas presented in the poetry of the song. Place the students in small groups, and have them imagine they are the producers of a music video. Using magazine pictures and their own drawings, have each group create a storyboard of images that would accompany the song in their video. Have the groups share their visions for the video with the class.

"WE ALL HAVE SONGS"

MUSIC & LYRICS BY JULIE SHANNON

© 1991 BY JULIE SHANNON

The lines in a face
Tell a story.
The lines in a face
Sing a song.
The lines are a keepsake
Of moments gone by,
Choices we've made,
Right or wrong.

And we earn our lines
From our stories.
We earn our lines
From our songs.
Trace the patterns,
And our stories unwind.
Who we are
Is in the lines
Left behind.

We all have songs.
We all have stories.
We all have good times
And times when
Things go wrong.
And that's life—
The heartache and the glory.

The heartbeat of life
Is in our stories and our songs.

A smooth young face
Holds a promise
Of stories that are waiting
To be told:
Places for laughter,
For tears to be cried,
Places for life to unfold.

And an aged face
Holds a treasure
That only the seekers shall find.
And is anybody there
To learn the song
That the music of a life
Might be passed along?

We all have songs.
We all have stories.
We all have good times
And times when
Things go wrong.
And that's life—
The heartache and the glory.
The heartbeat of life
Is in our stories and our songs.

And the melodies begin
In a baby's first cry.
And the harmonies blend in
As the years
Go passing by.

We sing the songs.
We tell the stories.
We sing of good times
And times when things go wrong.
So that life—
The heartache and the glory—
May long be remembered
In our stories and our songs.
The heartbeat of life
Is in our stories and our songs.
The heartbeat of life
Is in our stories and our songs.

For information about sheet music and a recording of this song, please contact Julie Shannon, Louisa May Alleycat Music, 2116 Thornwood Ave., Wilmette, IL 60091-1452, (847) 256-0112.

MAKING STORIES

Grade Level: 7–12
Objective: To introduce storytelling
Materials Needed: Kate D'Erasmo's "Making Stories"
Procedure: Share the poem with your students. Ask them to recall early storytelling experiences. Do they feel the same as the author of the poem? How might they recapture the joy of storytelling?

MAKING STORIES

Kate D'Erasmo

At times when words are hard to find,
I return to a high-ceilinged room, first row, third seat.

Everyone there is just seven. Miss Stone stands center stage.
We are all making stories about rain.

Drenched from a spring shower, weather words dance in our heads.
Trading storm clouds for visions, our lives change forever.

It began with connections and in building word-bridges:
We discovered small secrets hidden between.

Breathing life into stories gave needed permission
to seek possibility in ordinary things.

From that second grade classroom, spinning drops into wonder,
child-as-chameleon blossomed to writer.

Of late when it's raining, an old feeling reminds me,
since then making stories has not been the same.

From Kate D'Erasmo, in *Language Arts*, 67(2): 190. Copyright © 1990 by the National Council of Teachers of English. Reprinted with permission.

TELL ME A STORY

Grade Level: K–6
Objective: To introduce storytelling
Materials Needed: Copy of "Tell Me a Story" for each student
Procedure: Have students sing the song together. Ask them if they remember having their parents tell them stories. Discuss why storytelling is important. What are its values?

Chorus: Tell me a story, take me away,
It's too soon to sleep and I'm too tired to play,

Verse: When you were little, what did you do?
Tell me a story that's all about you.

Find me a castle, find me a bird,

Find me a story that I've never heard.

I am a captain who sails on the sea,

Tell me a story that's all about me.

I'm gonna get cranky if you don't come soon,

Let's take a story and fly to the moon.

From *Just Enough to Make a Story* (Berkeley, CA: Sisters' Choice Recordings & Books). Words and music by Nancy Schimmel. Copyright © 1983 by Nancy Schimmel. Used by permission. All rights reserved.

THE BEST OF ALL STORIES

Grade Level: 9–12
Objective: To understand that all of us have stories to tell
Materials Needed: Copy of "The Best of All Stories" for each student
Procedure: Have students read "The Best of All Stories." Ask students to write their autobiographies. These could be "bound" into a book. Illustrations, photos, memorabilia could be included. Students could choose an incident or anecdote from their autobiographies to share with classmates. If possible, create a storytelling program and invite parents for "An Evening of Autobiographies."

THE BEST OF ALL STORIES

James E. Birren

"Life can only be understood backwards; but it must be lived forwards." I use this quotation from Kierkegaard in my classes to emphasize the idea that people gain understanding by looking backward through autobiography. As I like to tell my classes, you don't know where you are going unless you know where you have been. In moving on from school into our later lives—career, career changes, marriage, divorce, retirement—we wonder, "Who am I?" We search for a self, an identity that is more than the membership and credit cards we carry with us. In the hurrying and often bruising experiences of life, our uniqueness can get squeezed out like toothpaste from a tube, making us feel empty and discarded.

In more than 40 years of studying adult development and aging, I have found that writing about our own life experiences and sharing them with others is one of the best ways we have of giving new meaning to our present lives by understanding our past more fully. For the past 11 years I have been teaching about the process and values of autobiography in universities and in workshops at gerontology meetings and conferences in this country and abroad.

Writing an autobiography puts the contradictions, paradoxes and ambivalence of life into perspective. It restores our sense of self-sufficiency and personal identity that has been shaped by the crosscurrents and tides of life. I remember the sense of freedom that Marcus had when he wrote and later told the group, "I come from a family of slobs. Even my father's brother cheated him." In such comments the listener grasps the meaning of being a part of such a background, as well as what it means to rise above it.

Carole wrote that when she was in high school her father told her that she was so smart that if she had been a boy he would have sent her to medical school. Now, in retirement, she accepts the dual reality—of being a woman and being smart—that in her earlier life had made her uncertain and ambivalent.

A tornado blew away the house in which Margaret lived with her family as a child. "I had to go to work when I was 12," she wrote. "It didn't help matters that my father had a great temper and kept losing his job." Writing an autobiography, at age 75, helped her find peace in her life.

My interest in autobiography began in a summer class I taught at the University of Hawaii 11 years ago. Every day I assigned a paper on some topic in the field of adult development and aging. One day, as a change of pace, I gave my students an unusual assignment: Write two or three pages telling about your life as if it were a tree and describing its major branching points. Or think of your life as a river and tell how it flowed, taking a new path here and being dammed up there, narrowing and widening with events.

The next day's class was startling. The students all wanted to talk at once. Somehow I had pressed a button and the class was alive in a way that I had rarely seen.

The excitement made me think of how autobiography has been neglected in psychology. After working with a group of graduate students for a year to explore autobiography, I introduced a course, Psychological Development Through Guided Autobiography, for graduate students, advanced undergraduates, professionals and retired persons. We met three hours a day for two weeks. The participants became so engrossed that many of them didn't want to stop writing their autobiographies when the course ended. On the last day of class they brought food for lunch and exchanged addresses and promises to remain in touch. Some members of this and later groups have had reunions to update their autobiographies.

After helping hundreds of people write their autobiographies, the most important thing I have learned confirms Hemingway's observation that "the world breaks everyone and afterward many are strong at the broken places." I tell each of my classes, "You are all survivors. Tell us your story and we will tell you ours." I don't tell them how strong I think they are, since that is part of the process of individual discovery. In reviewing the details of their lives people become impressed with all the problems they have survived, and the many ways they have been tested by events and by people.

You too will be amazed at the amount of detail you remember when you write an autobiography and share it with others. As the names of places and people come bubbling up, along with the events of yesterday—your first crush, your first job—they take on a new complexion and order. Your life becomes a tapestry, and the actions of the past seem to form a pattern.

The autobiographical process doesn't stop with the recalling and writing. You understand your life better if you share it piece by piece with other people. That is why I always have a class break up into small groups of three to six each. Everybody reads aloud the two pages or so they have written on a particular theme, such as the role of money in their lives or their work histories.

Something happens during the reading that goes beyond what is achieved by the writing alone. Paradoxically, some things that seem difficult to write about alone are easily expressed in a group. New associations arise from the group discussion. The facts and the feelings take on a living quality for both readers and listeners as each new session builds on previous sessions. Other people's experiences become reminders of feelings and events that we have set aside and thought we had forgotten.

Autobiography is most useful when it is guided. A good guide is like the old fisherman who always seemed to catch fish when others, with good equipment and the right bait, came back empty-handed. Asked why, he said, "I know where the fish are." One good fishing spot for significant autobiographical materials is family history. But there are others, such as the history of our health and body, how we got into our life's work, our experiences with death, our loves and our hates. Merely mentioning these topics can set off a train of rich associations.

Along with the emotional recall of an early loss or a broken love relationship, there are often humorous recollections. Humor in an autobiography is an indication that the writer has mastered a problem. As people become more experienced with the autobiographical process, humor becomes more frequent. Its use suggests that the person has moved from seeing life as a series of problems to greater insight and mastery.

An apt metaphor is also useful in understanding one's life. "Trade in and trade up the old metaphors that you use to characterize yourselves," I tell the class. "I have been a pussycat all of my life, but now I am becoming a tigress," one woman said with a smile, and the group smiled with her. The important can be made funny and acceptable and the complex can be grasped through the right metaphor.

I am constantly impressed by the durability of memories. The clarity with which many 80-year-olds describe early life events can be awesome. The hidden pranks and sibling rivalries of 50 years ago are recalled with the freshness of yesterday. Long-term memories don't seem to fade or become lost; they are awaiting our attention. Sensitizing ourselves to finding the old memories is one of the advantages of doing guided autobiography in a group.

It is surprising that while we spend so much money and effort on cemeteries for dead bodies, we have so little interest in archives for living autobiographies. But the current popularity of biographies and autobiographies shows there is a rising interest in a search for the meaning of our lives amid the ambiguities of the transition from an industrial society to the information age, from the pencil and typewriter to the computer and the nuclear age.

Why not start tomorrow to tell yourself and others the story of your life, and "understand it backwards"? It may help to join a local adult-education class on autobiography or get a "how-to-do-it" book from the library to guide you. Having a friend who will write and share as you go along will keep the process moving.

I've found that we feel stronger and more hopeful after writing and sharing our autobiographies. We see that we must have been good travelers to have gotten this far. Sharing with others the autobiographical road map of your life, its potholes, rest areas, vistas and flat tires, leads to new bonds, ones that often are surprisingly durable. Many of my former students tell me doing their autobiographies was one of the most significant experiences of their lives. Let us get on with the telling of the best stories of all, our own stories.

Reprinted with permission from *Psychology Today Magazine* 5: 91–92. Copyright © 1987 (Sussex Publishers, Inc.)

IT'S BEEN MY EXPERIENCE THAT...

Grade Level: K–12 (depending on topic choice)
Objective: To motivate storytelling about personal experiences
Procedure: Ask students to create stories around the following list of personal experiences. Have students tell the stories.

"When I grow up, I want to ..."
"The scariest thing that ever happened to me was ..."
"My grandfather is the best ..."
"The event from my childhood I remember most vividly is ..."
"If I could live my life over, the event I would change would be ..."
"The best thing that ever happened to me is ..."
"The origin of my last name is ..."

RITUAL OBJECTS

Grade Level: 7–12
Objective: To personalize storytelling through students' own ritual
Materials Needed: Hats, all kinds of wearing apparel, necklaces, sticks, aprons, bags, baskets, ropes, or imaginary objects that "see" stories, "hold" stories, or "indicate" stories
Procedure: Lead students in the following:

Have the teller adopt a ritual object to hold stories, to identify stories, or to act as a storytelling talisman of good luck. Richard Chase uses a walking stick and a bag. Jackie Torrence wears an unusual medallion. Spencer Shaw lights a candle before storytelling and blows it out at the end. Greg Denman uses a stool and a hat. John Stansfield carries a woven knapsack. Opalanga Pugh shakes her gourd rattle. Sandra Rietz wears a special vest. Pam Cooper wears a storytelling doll pendant.

As students develop their storytelling talents, encourage them to add a ritual object to their personal storytelling habit. Tell them that it may take experience with several ideas before they find the "right" object for them.

Adapted from Norma Livo and Sandra Rietz, *Storytelling Activities,* p. 50 (Littleton, CO: Libraries Unlimited, 1987). Used by permission.

STORYTELLER'S CREED

Grade Level: 7–12

Objective: To state what storytelling should be

Procedure: Have students create their own storytelling creeds. The one below comes from Robert Fulghum, *All I Really Need to Know I Learned in Kindergarten.*

I believe that imagination is stronger than knowledge.
That myth is more potent than history.
That dreams are more powerful than facts.
That hope always triumphs over experience.
That laughter is the only cure for grief.
And I believe that love is stronger than death.

From *All I Really Need to Know I Learned in Kindergarten* by Robert Fulghum. Copyright © 1986, 1988 by Robert L. Fulghum. Reprinted by permission of Villard Books, a division of Random House, Inc.

NO SUCH THINGS

Grade Level: 3–12

Objective: To stimulate the imagination

Materials Needed: Bill Peet's *No Such Things* (Boston: Houghton Mifflin, 1983)

Procedure: Using rhythmic verse, Bill Peet has created a picture book full of creatures that amuse and delight listeners and readers (see example below). Each of these descriptions of fanciful creatures is accompanied by Peet's fanciful crayon illustrations. After hearing several of these verses, have students create their own fanciful characters and illustrate them. These creations could be bound into a group book of their own No Such Things. Students also could make up stories about their fanciful creature and share the stories with other class members.

If the fancy Fandangos seem stuck-up and snooty,
It is mostly because of their exquisite beauty.
They're most often seen with smug smiling faces,
By a crystal clear pond in a jungle oasis.

From Norma Livo and Sandra Rietz, in *Storytelling Activities*, p. 9 (Littleton, CO: Libraries Unlimited, 1987). Used by permission.

. . . .

IMAGINE THAT!

Grade Level: 7–12
Objective: To strengthen imagination
Materials Needed: Imagination Assignment Sheet, Imagination Activity Sheet, and Imagination Critique Sheet
Procedure: Give the students the Imagination Assignment Sheet and the Imagination Activity Sheet. Use the Imagination Critique Sheet to critique the improvised scenes.

IMAGINATION ASSIGNMENT SHEET

Here is a chance to let your imagination flow freely. You and two other classmates, working as a group, are to improvise a five-minute scene around three unrelated words. As soon as you select the group of words, set your imagination to word and incorporate the words as an integral part of a fantastic scene that your group can play. As you improvise, your imagination will help supply the dialogue and action.

You will be graded on how uniquely you work the words into a scene and how far-fetched the situation is. You will be graded also on your concentration in maintaining character and developing the scene.

How to prepare

Your instructor will group you with two other classmates. Together you are to pick a series of three unrelated words. The following are suggestions:

toothbrush, horse, earring

paper clip, telephone, baked potato

pizza, Duke, typewriter

lamp, rifle, zipper

rug, zebra, rosebush

paint brush, parsnips, dishwasher

trumpet, sea shell, tractor

aspirin, diamonds, cactus

cookie jar, snow shovel, swimming suit

door knob, newspaper, monkey

spoon, dice, bathtowel

patio, haystack, elevator

angle worm, boxing gloves, postage stamp

mink coat, shovel, toaster

compass, rabbit, dictionary

your own choice

You will be allowed 40 minutes in class for planning and rehearsing the scene. Using your combined imaginations, create a strange situation in which three words play an integral part as important objects. Be sure that the association of the articles is fantastic and that your story contains much action (movement you can do). Plan the basic sequence of action, arranging the scene for completion within four to five minutes. You may play yourself in the situation or you may assume a different person. Either way, be sure you "stay in character" by concentrating on what that person would say and do in that particular situation.

Suppose your group selects the following words: eraser, ladder, cabbage. You might concoct a story like this:

> You are a governess to a ten-year-old girl who receives a letter saying that she will receive, within the week, a large sum of candy left her by a wealthy old uncle. The only stipulation is that the child must have long, pointed ears before she can receive the goodies. Hoping to make the child's ears longer, you attach a string to them, tie the string to a door knob, and pull the child away from the door. This doesn't work. Her ears remain the same.
>
> Frantically, you take the child to a noted German psychologist. After referring to his large book, he finds the formula for growing ears: Eat a special rabbit's diet, which consists of art-gum eraser bits and three drops of cabbage juice.
>
> The child eagerly writes a letter and then erases it to obtain the art-gum eraser scraps. To secure the cabbage juice, the child is instructed to climb a tall ladder and to drop a cabbage head into a bucket. This she does three times, to obtain the three drops of juice. Each time she drops it, you and the doctor say loudly, "Gesundheit."
>
> The child descends the ladder, eats the food, and her ears begin to grow. Soon they are long and pointed like those of a rabbit. She is elated, but suddenly she begins to feel strange, and in a few seconds she quickly turns into a rabbit, hopping out of the office with you and the doctor pursuing her.

Outline the improvisation, using the Imagination Activity Sheet. Be sure that each of you knows the sequence of the planned story. Also decide which of you will announce the scene in class.

How to present

When your group is called upon, hand your Imagination Activity Sheet to your teacher and go quietly to the playing area. Two of you may arrange needed chairs and tables, while the third may write the three words on the board, and then announce the scene to the class.

With vivid imagination, improvise the scene following the basic planned situation as rehearsed, but making up words and action as you play. Be sure you stay within the four- to five-minute time limit.

IMAGINATION ACTIVITY SHEET

On this sheet, construct a neat, complete sentence outline of your improvised scene situation. Hand to your instructor before performing.

Name ....

Type of Activity ....

List unrelated words to be used ....

Setting ....

Character you are going to be ....

Situation: (Outline step by step. Include ample action.)

    I. Introduction:

    II. Body:

    III. Conclusion:

IMAGINATION CRITIQUE SHEET

Student's Name ....

Instructor's Comments:

Created a unique and active scene from the word association:

Maintained concentration (stayed within character and situation):

Contributed to scene development:

Additional suggestions:

Adapted from Fran Tanner, *Basic Drama Projects,* 5th ed., pp. 30–31, 33–34 (Caldwell, ID: Clark Publishing, 1987). Used by permission.

GUIDED FANTASY

Grade Level: 7–12

Objective: To practice visualization

Procedure: Use a gentling or relaxation exercise before getting into guided fantasy experiences. Then talk the listeners through the outline of a fantasy that is structured in such a way that the listeners must fill in the blanks and use their imaginations. While guiding the experience, include pauses for developing the inner imaginative thinking of the participants. The actual guided story (not including pauses) should probably last five minutes. During this time, each listener should feel a sense of having either experienced a dream while awake or having lived through a novel.

Within the guided fantasy, leave blanks for listeners to recall buried childhood memories and stories. Favorite places are also good to include.

A sample fantasy

"You are about to go on a trip. Get yourself relaxed and comfortable. Close your eyes.

"Imagine that you are in the place that you love most. (Pause) Where is this place? What does it smell like? What memories do you have of this place? Why is it your favorite place? You leave this place and start out on a trip. (Pause) Where are you going? Who and what will you see when you get there? What will you take with you for this trip? You get there and experience the most joyful experience you ever had. (Pause) What was that experience? What made it so joyful for you? Did others realize what was happening? What did you do after it? And now, you are being whisked up in the air by a gentle, cool breeze. (Pause) Where does it take you? What happens when you get there? Does your story end there?

"Now, slowly come back to where you are now. Open your eyes."

You may ask for volunteers to share their stories. As people share, others may be reminded of similar thoughts. They have all, if they have concentrated, brought back warm stories from their past. Our memories are invisible cargo that we all carry with us wherever we go.

From Norma Livo and Sandra Rietz, *Storytelling Activities*, pp. 14–15. (Littleton, CO: Libraries Unlimited, 1987). Used by permission.

SPONTANEOUS CREATIVITY

Grade Level: 3–6

Objective: To understand that creative thinking derives from the ability not only to look, but to see; not only to hear, but to listen; not only to imitate, but to innovate; not only to observe, but to experience the excitement of fresh perception.

Materials Needed: Slips of paper with unusual character, problem, and setting ideas.

Procedure: Prepare (or have students prepare) unusual character, problem, and setting ideas. Write them on slips of paper and place them in boxes marked "Character," "Problem," "Setting." Ask students to take turns drawing an idea from each box and developing a spontaneous story using the selected idea.

Examples

Character	Problem	Setting
giant	storm	in a forest
mosquito	amnesia	in the desert
anteater	need for money	up Jack's beanstalk
beaver	lost	on a horse
fairy godmother	nearsighted	in Africa

From Norma Livo and Sandra Rietz, *Storytelling Activities*, pp. 4–5. (Littleton, CO: Libraries Unlimited, 1987). Used by permission.

LITERARY NEWS REPORT

Grade Level: K–6

Objective: To focus on important details

Procedure: Working with familiar stories, introduce the idea of a literary news report by composing television or radio newscast reports using the pattern found in such broadcasts:

Opening Announcement: Must catch your attention and tell you what happened.

Place and Date: Tells where the story came from and when it happened.

On the Scene: First sentence sums up the headline and may add more detail.

Detailed Account:	Answers the questions: Who? What? When? Where? How? Why? Include quotations from eyewitnesses.

Example

Opening Announcement:	Woodcutter rescues Little Red Riding Hood.
Place and Date:	South Branch of Forest; Wednesday; and so on.

A variation on this theme would be a newspaper report.

LITERARY INTERVIEWS

Grade Level:	K–6
Objective:	To take the perspective of a character
Procedure:	In the literary interview have one or more students take on the role of a character from a story. Introduce this routine by coaching the child in a character role and then by acting as interviewer yourself. Elicit from children the importance of the interviewer's asking good questions. At first, questions should be based on concrete story information. The questions can then relate to events that happened "before" or "after" the story. Continue in this vein.

Example

Interviewer:	Good morning, boys and girls. This morning we have a lucky Little Red Riding Hood with us. I understand you had a very harrowing experience involving a wolf. Could you tell us about it?

A LITTLE CONCENTRATION

Grade Level:	3–6
Objective:	To increase concentration skills
Procedure:	Have students complete the following:

1. Divide the class into circles of about 15 people each. One person says one word; the second person repeats that word and then adds a different word that she associates with the first (example: butter, followed by bread). Continue adding words around the circle. Students forgetting a word must drop out.

2. Choose a situation in which you can play yourself and in which you are about to do something. Briefly describe the situation to the class, then, improvise out loud what your thoughts would be. For example, you have

been called into the dean's office at school and are in the outer room waiting for the dean's door to open. Verbalize your thoughts, fears, and hopes.

3. With a partner, start an argument involving both of you. Talk simultaneously and without pause, each developing and keeping your mind on your own reasons. Example lines to initiate argument: "You were driving too fast," "You're late," "Turn off that TV!"

Adapted from Fran Tanner, *Basic Drama Projects*, 5th ed., p. 20 (Caldwell, ID: Clark Publishing, 1987). Used by permission.

CLOSE OBSERVATION REVEALS THAT . . .

Grade Level: 7–12

   Objective: To increase observation skills

   Procedure: Have students complete the following activities:

1. Choose a gathering of people that seems interesting to you—at a farm auction, a political rally, a bargain sale, a child's playground, a fair, a city bus, a hotel lobby, a night at the theatre, an airport, etc. Mingle with the people. Observe them. Select one person who appears unique. Concentrate on his movement, facial expression, behavior. In class, reproduce that person's movement, posture, gestures, etc. Try to be exact in showing what you observed and in indicating why the person was acting that particular way.

2. Choose an age group—childhood, teenage, middle age, old age—and note basic movements indicative of that group. Your observations should include movement of the body, head, legs, arms. Discover a rhythmic beat that you would associate with that age. In class, enact the age group you studied, first silently, and then again with a musical background on record that suggests the rhythm you noted. (Select the record carefully before class and rehearse with it at home.)

3. Choose an animal that impresses you, and study its movements and rhythm. How does the animal handle its body, its front paws, back paws, head? Notice its eyes, claws, tail, and any other identifying factors. Act out the animal in class. If your portrayal is exact, the class should be able to guess correctly the animal you are portraying. (This would be appropriate for grades K–3.)

4. Do the mirror exercise. Divide into pairs of A and B. Face each other, looking directly into your partner's eyes. Partner A initiates slow movement of arms, hands, and body, as though he/she were under water, using space around him/her. B is the mirror and must reflect exactly all of A's activities and facial expressions. At a command from your teacher, reverse your roles, with A being the mirror. Communicate with your eyes. Strive to work together, trying not to trick your partner with quick movements. Later add voice sound.

Adapted from Fran Tanner, *Basic Drama Projects*, 5th ed., p. 14 (Caldwell, ID: Clark Publishing, 1987). Used by permission.

THINGS AREN'T ALWAYS WHAT THEY SEEM

Grade Level: K–3

Objective: To reinforce the concept of point of view

Procedure: Read to students *The True Story of the Three Little Pigs,* by A. Wolf as told to Jon Scieszka (New York: Penguin Books, 1989). Ask them to retell a fairytale from another character's point of view. For example: *Cinderella* from the stepmother's, *Goldilocks and the Three Bears* from the baby bear's, *Jack and the Beanstalk* from the giant's. Discuss how the story changes as the point of view changes.

COMING TO OUR SENSES

Grade Level: 7–12

Objective: To strengthen sense recall

Procedure: Have students complete several of the following:

1. Choose a category such as flowers, beverages, cups, fruit. Outside of class, observe four different types of objects within the genre you have chosen. Note the similarities and differences. For example, how do you handle a china tea cup, a coffee mug, a tin cup, a small demitasse cup? Or how does the taste of milk, tea, orange juice, and hot chocolate differ? In class, recall the sense impression of each article and pantomime your contact with each. Attempt honestly to recall the actual sensation as you pantomime. Feel the china cup in your hand, or taste the tart, pulpy orange juice as it trickles down your throat.

2. Choose an activity that can occur in various situations. For example: walking in sand, mud, rain, snow; or carrying a suitcase that is heavy, empty, bulky. Observe how you would walk in the various elements, or how you would carry the different suitcases. Let all your senses give you a strong impression. Then recall that impression as you pantomime the activities.

3. Divide into groups of four or five, with each group choosing a simple item to "eat." In turn, each group goes to the front of the room and proceeds to "taste," "smell," and "eat" the imaginary food. Work on recalling the real food as you eat it.

4. Divide into groups, each deciding a sporting event to watch as a group. Go to the front of the room and observe the sport, "seeing" it with your whole body.

Adapted from Fran Tanner, *Basic Drama Projects,* 5th ed., pp. 25–26 (Caldwell, ID: Clark Publishing, 1987). Used by permission.

STORYTELLING WARM-UP IDEAS

Grade Level: 7–12

Objective: To develop the skill of inventiveness and the ability to see new relationships

Materials Needed: Cards with ideas

Procedure: Put the following ideas on cards; have students draw a card, work with the idea on it, and then present it to the class.

1. Imagine that you are an object. Be that object, and tell a story from the object's point of view.

2. Recall a personal experience using sensory recall. How did things/people look, smell, feel, taste? What sounds and colors were there? Was it hot or cold? Tell about it.

3. What is the earliest personal experience you can remember? How old were you? Where were you? What happened?

4. Create three characters. Put them in a conflict situation. Tell the story of how the conflict was resolved.

5. Concentrate on observing an object for 10 minutes. Take no notes. Afterward, write details that describe the object. (This is a good exercise for heightened awareness.)

6. Compose a short story that includes an obscure word. Use the story or pun to teach that vocabulary word. A good source of ideas is *The Weighty Word Book,* by Paul M. Levitt, Douglas A. Burger, and Elissa S. Guralnick (1985).

7. Draw a picture or sculpt a character from a story you have heard. Be as detailed as possible.

8. Use the phrase, "No I won't do it," and present it to show anger, boredom, irritation, grief, surprise, joy, fright, shyness, slyness. Have the class guess each mood you are expressing.

9. For two people: Create a story about a phrase or thing chosen by your partner.

Adapted from Norma Livo and Sandra Rietz, *Storytelling Activities,* p. 7 (Littleton, CO: Libraries Unlimited, 1987). Used by permission.

THE LIAR'S CONTEST

Grade Level: 6–12

Objective: To share true stories in small groups and make someone else's story your own, trying to convince others that the events really occurred to you.

Procedure: Have students complete the following:

1. Divide students into groups of four. Assign each group a topic for storytelling and invite each student to tell a true story from his own life concerning the topic. Give each small group a period of time to share short stories from its memories with each other. Sample topics are:

   something that happened with an animal

   a time you felt scared

   something that happened at a birthday party

   a time you felt embarrassed

   something that happened with a best or worst teacher

   something that happened on a vacation

2. Ask each group to choose one of the four stories. Invite the teller of this story to tell it again. This time, listeners in the group may stop her to ask questions. Then have each member of the group prepare the story as if it really happened to her. The task is to create a first-person telling so convincing that listeners will think it is a true story. Invite a group to come before the class and have the four tellers sit in a line. Each one is to tell the story in his own words as if the events really happened to him. Finally have the class vote (perhaps by applause) as to who is telling the truth. After the vote, the teller reveals himself, and the class can discuss elements of believable storytelling.

VOICE WARM-UP

Grade Level: All

Objective: To get the voice ready for storytelling

Procedure: Give students any of the following directions to get the voice warmed up before storytelling.

1. Tongue twisters: Say quickly, with exaggerated tongue, lip, and jaw movements, several of the following tongue twisters:

   Two teamsters tried to steal twenty-two keys.

   Would Wheeler woo Wanda if Woody snoozed woozily?

   Much whirling water makes the mill wheel work well.

   Odd birds always gobble green almonds in the autumn.

   She makes a proper cup of coffee in a copper coffee pot.

2. Smile-pucker: Smile with exaggeration, letting your teeth show and drawing the lips as tightly as possible, making your cheek muscles hurt. Say, "eeeeeeee." Then, with exaggeration, pucker or protrude your lips, saying "oooooooo." Repeat ten times each in quick succession (eeeeeeee-oooooooo). Repeat with "me-moo," "tee-too," "bee-boo," "gee-goo," and "lee-loo."

3. Saying "ahhhhhhhh," sustain a comfortable pitched tone. Intone loud, then softer; higher, then lower.

4. Gibberish: You and a partner carry on an animated conversation simultaneously with the rest of the class by using gibberish, which consists of nonsense or make-believe words. If you find it difficult at first to think up non-words, simply use only the term "da-da-shoon." Sincerely try to communicate.

5. Singing: Energetically carry on an argument with your partner by "singing" your sentences as is done in opera. You needn't carry a tune. Just go up and down the scale according to what you think fits your ideas and words; the more exaggerated, the better.

6. Say a sentence such as "Now is the time," or "Everything is different," or "There goes the last one," in each of the following ways: sternly, frightened, eagerly, defiantly, soothingly, shyly, dubiously, drowsily, wistfully, joyfully, airily, ominously, irritably, stunned, sadly, happily, nostalgically, remorsefully.

7. Say "What are you doing?" as though you were:

   a wild person

   just learning to read

   talking to a cute puppy

   a preacher

   talking to a deaf person

   a police officer

   dictating to a secretary

   a frightened child

8. Count from one to ten in the following ways:

   counting pennies on a table

   counting out a fighter in a boxing ring

   counting people in a crowded room

   counting off in an exercise routine

Adapted from Fran Tanner, *Basic Drama Projects*, 5th ed., p. viii (Caldwell, ID: Clark Publishing, 1987). Used by permission.

TWELVE TERRIBLE TONGUE TWISTERS TO TEST TELLERS' TALENTS

Grade Level: All

Objective: To get the voice ready for storytelling

Procedure: Have students say the following as fast as they can:

1. Free Tree Twigs.
   Free Tree Twigs.
   Free Tree Twigs.

2. Delicious suspicious spaghetti.
   Delicious suspicious spaghetti.
   Delicious suspicious spaghetti.

3. Slime shuns sunshine.
   Slime shuns sunshine.
   Slime shuns sunshine.

4. Did Moses suppose his toes were a rose?
   Did Moses suppose his toes were a rose?
   Did Moses suppose his toes were a rose?

5. Tom the terrible teacher taught tots naughty thoughts.
   Tom the terrible teacher taught tots naughty thoughts.
   Tom the terrible teacher taught tots naughty thoughts.

6. Betty Botter bought a bit of better butter. But the bit of better butter
   Betty Botter bought was a bit bitter for better butter.

7. No need to light a night light on a light night like tonight.
   No need to light a night light on a light night like tonight.

8. We won by one run.
   We won by one run.
   We won by one run.

9. Caesar seized his knees and sneezed.
   Caesar seized his knees and sneezed.
   Caesar seized his knees and sneezed.

10. A manager of an imaginary menagerie.
    A manager of an imaginary menagerie.
    A manager of an imaginary menagerie.

11. The pleased police released the leash.
    The pleased police released the leash.
    The pleased police released the leash.

12. The sixth sick sheik's sixth sheep is sick.
    The sixth sick sheik's sixth sheep is sick.
    The sixth sick sheik's sixth sheep is sick.

From John Moschitta, "Motor Mouth," *Hilarious Tongue Twister Game* (Vernon Hills, IL: Tiger Games, 1990). Used by permission.

MOVE LIKE I MOVE

Grade Level: All

Objective: To develop body awareness

Procedure: Read a fairytale to students, for example, "Cinderella." Divide students into small groups. Have each student pantomime different actions. For example, how would the stepsisters stand? How would Cinderella mop the floor after she learns she can't go to the ball? What kind of movements would a fairy godmother use? Ask students to discuss why they selected the movements they did.

BODY WARM-UPS

Grade Level: All

Objective: To get the body loosened up for storytelling

Procedure: Give students any of the following directions prior to their storytelling performances:

1. Rag doll: With feet apart in a comfortable balance, stretch up tall. Then bend over by collapsing quickly and loosely from the waist with your relaxed arms and hands dangling to the floor. Keep your arms, hands, and head completely relaxed like a rag doll. Slowly rise up, keeping relaxed. Repeat.

2. Head roll: Immediately after the rag doll exercise, while your neck is still relaxed with chin close to the chest, slowly rotate your head to the left, back, right, and down in front again. Reverse the rotation. Be sure to keep your neck relaxed, letting your head roll like a dead weight in a socket.

3. Arm swing: Immediately after the head roll, swing relaxed arms in large circles, one at a time.

4. Numbers: Using your whole body, write huge numbers from one to ten in the air. Use as much space as you can, traveling around the room, stretching and bending as you write. If possible, do this to slow, relaxing music.

5. Tug of war: With a team of six to twelve, form a line by standing in front of each other and facing a similarly placed and numbered team. With an imaginary rope, play tug of war, trying to get the rope away from the other side. See and feel the rope. Make it so real in your mind that at the end of the game you will be tired from the great physical exertion.

Adapted from Fran Tanner, *Basic Drama Projects,* 5th ed., p. viii (Caldwell, ID: Clark Publishing, 1987). Used by permission.

• •

LET'S GET MOTIVATED!

Grade Level: 3–12

  Objective: To understand that all movement must be motivated

  Procedure: Have students choose an activity that they can do easily and choose a character who may do that action. The following are suggestions:

Character suggestions

Elderly lady, soldier, farmer, butler, police officer, salesperson, athlete, hobo, gardener, scientist, congressperson, miser, child, teacher, chauffeur, dancer, student's own choice.

Activity suggestions

Doing exercises, flying a kite, washing a car, bridling a horse, picking a bouquet, typing a letter, chopping wood, shoveling snow, doing dishes, washing windows, shaking rugs, rollerblading, doing embroidery, learning to drive a car.

Scene example

You are an elderly man who needs money to buy food. You have been hired to dig out dandelions in a lady's yard. You want to do a good job so that she will hire you back to do more yard work. As you dig carefully, feel the implement in your hand. See the dandelions; visualize the yard and house. Feel the sunshine beat down on your head. As you work, you grow thirsty and tired. How you would like a drink of water! But you keep on working, your action justified by your wish to do a good job so that you will be rehired.

Ask students to determine the type of person your character is: personality, background, age, appearance, etc.; the circumstances leading up to the scene; and the character's motivating desire or wishes in that scene.

Have students rehearse a two- to three-minute scene by concentrating on the reason they are doing the action. Explain: Forget yourself and the way you do the action. In real life you are seldom as concerned with how you do something as you are with why you are doing it. For example, you are cleaning your room because you want to impress your grandmother who is visiting you; you are hoeing the garden because you can't have the car until you are through; you are painting a fence because you need to earn money for a new CD.

As students rehearse, have them use sensory recall to visualize the situation. Tell students to "see" the fence they are painting, "smell" the paint, "feel" the brush in their hand, etc.

Have students rehearse by saying their character's thoughts aloud. This will help them concentrate on the purpose of the action.

Have students perform their scenes.

Adapted from Fran Tanner, *Basic Drama Projects*, 5th ed., pp. 60–61 (Caldwell, ID: Clark Publishing, 1987). Used by permission.

• •

PRESENTING SCENES FROM STORY

Grade Level: K–6
  Objective: To gain skill by using body and dialogue to create story
  Procedure: Select and read a story to the class, and then move to a spacious area such as the gymnasium and have the children act out various parts of the story.

Directions for scenes to act out could follow the chronological sequence of the story, but there's no need to act out every event. The children's pantomime could be planned or improvised. A variation on this theme would be to introduce children to different dramatic situations that arise in narrative before they are familiar with a given story.

Example

The wolf is skulking through the dense woods when he sees and smells a little girl with a red hood carrying a basket of goodies. Be the skulking wolf meeting the little girl.

• •

THE WORD'S THE THING

Grade Level: 7–12
  Objective: To refine narrative description
  Procedure: Have students keep a "word journal" in which they write down words, phrases, proverbs, sayings, and any speech uses they find particularly funny, dramatic, musical, or beautiful. Ask them to work some of what they've written into their stories.

• •

SKELETON STORIES

Grade Level: K–6
    Objective: To enable students to create their own stories
    Procedure: Make up stories using the skeletal framework of props, charac-
          ters, or settings to stimulate ideas. Motivation will be enhanced
          if you have the props on hand along with pictures of the char-
          acters and settings. Experiment with combining the categories,
          too. Endless possibilities exist for this activity.

Examples

    Props: A miniature broom, a piece of jewelry, a decorative box
    Characters: A witch, a king, a clown
    Settings: Haunted house, schoolyard, castle

From Ruth Beall Heinig, *Creative Drama Resource Book: For Grades 4 through 6*, p. 138. Copyright ©
1987 by Prentice-Hall, Englewood Cliffs, NJ. Used by permission.

• •

STORY TRUNK

Grade Level: K–3
    Objective: To create an illusion of an object
    Procedure: "Drag" an imaginary trunk into the classroom. You might
          even ask students to help you drag it in. Tell students that
          in this trunk are many, many objects from a story. Ask each
          student to come up, take something from the story trunk,
          and pantomime how that object is used, who uses it, and when
          it is used. Students should then use the objects to create an
          original story.

Note: The story trunk can also be used in a storytelling performance. In this
case, the trunk is full of tiny, imaginary scrolls on which are written titles of
stories. Ask a student to reach into the trunk, pull out an imaginary scroll, and
hand it to you, the storyteller. You then unroll the scroll and tell whatever story
you wish, saying something like, "Oh, you have chosen the best story of all. It
is called...."

• •

VISUALIZE! VISUALIZE!

Grade Level: All

Objective: To develop the ability to visualize and to make action believable

Materials Needed: Pantomime Outline Form and Pantomime Critique Form

Procedure: Have students complete the following:

Have students choose an activity to pantomime. Some possibilities are: building a campfire, shining shoes, rowing a canoe, changing a flat tire, learning to rollerblade. Explain that students need to think about the action and see it in their minds. For example, if a student chooses to pantomime setting a table, he must "see" the room (the pictures on the wall, the size of the room, the placement of the table in relationship to doors and other pieces of furniture), the action: picking up the dishes, glasses, utensils, and so on and carrying them into the room, placing them on the table, feeling their weight as they are being carried, and setting each place correctly. Students should make everything they do believable.

Students should complete the Pantomime Outline Form and hand it to you before they perform their pantomimes. Pantomimes should be 1–3 minutes. Use the Pantomime Critique Form to critique the pantomimes.

Adapted from Fran Tanner, *Basic Drama Projects*, 5th ed., pp. 7–10 (Caldwell, ID: Clark Publishing, 1987). Used by permission.

PANTOMIME OUTLINE FORM

Construct a neat, complete sentence outline on this sheet. Hand it to your instructor when you rise to perform.

Name: ....

Activity you will pantomime: ....

Where pantomime takes place (kitchen, bowling alley, etc.): ....

....

Action: (Outline step by step)

I. Introduction:

II. Body:

III. Conclusion:

PANTOMIME CRITIQUE FORM

Name ....

1. Movement carefully executed:

    a.   Presented action in believable sequence ....

         ....

    b.   Paid attention to details ....

         ....

    c.   Followed through on all movement ....

         ....

2. Body response pliable and expressive ....

    ....

3. Pantomime believable ....

    ....

Additional suggestions:

WANTED POSTERS

Grade Level:	K–6
Objective:	To develop a character in the story
Materials Needed:	One of the best stories to use in this activity is Eric Kimmel's *Hershel and the Hanukkah Goblins* (New York: Scholastic, 1985, 1989).
Procedure:	Have students complete the following:

Have students make a wanted posted for Hershel or one of the goblins. The wanted poster should resemble the following: Dimensions should be no larger than 12" by 18". It should be clear, legible, and not on paper that is too dark to be readable. The poster should be done in ink or felt-tip pen. The poster should contain a sketch of the character. Students should find an offense that the character should be accused of or a virtue the character should be praised for.

The poster should contain the character's name and an alias. The poster should have a paragraph describing the offense and the trouble it has caused, or the virtue and the good it has caused. The paragraph should be about five sentences. Phrases such as, "She can be seen ... ," "He is usually found ...'" "Use extreme caution because ..." can be used.

A second paragraph of about three sentences should be included that provides a physical description of the character.

The reward for the character's capture should be something consistent with the offense or virtue. For example, if the offense is consistent tardiness, a watch might be the reward.

LITERARY POSTERS

Grade Level:	3–6
Objective:	To select significant details
Procedure:	Create a poster around some aspect of a story. Different types of literary posters might be:

- *Missing Person Poster:* Have you seen this character? List information from the story both implied and stated.
- *Suspect Identity Chart:* List the characteristics of the characters (human or non-human).

Example: Missing person poster

MISSING!!

Name: Little Red Riding Hood

Address:

Eyes:

Hair:

Height:

Clothing:

Features:

Habits:

Last Seen:

BUILDING CHARACTER

Grade Level: 7–12

Objective: To develop a clear characterization

Procedure: Below are several projects on characterization. Ask your students to complete several of them.

1. Select newspaper human interest stories. In groups, supply the necessary characters for the action. Analyze the characters. Then improvise a scene built around the printed story.

2. In groups, build a scene around a historical event such as Lewis and Clark's first meeting with Sacajawea, Madame Curie's discovery of radium, Alexander Graham Bell's first successful use of the telephone, etc. Be sure your story has dramatic value, a clearly defined plot, a climax.

3. Select a picture from a magazine or from a reproduction of a famous painting that shows an interesting looking person. Analyze that person in terms of what you see in the picture. In class, show the picture and report what feelings, thoughts, and behavior make this character distinctive.

4. Choose an external hand property or costume accessory such as a pair of white gloves, a colorful silk umbrella, a pocket watch, dangle bracelets, a battered hat, a nosegay of violets, a rusty pocket knife. Create a brief scene in which you portray a character suggested by the object.

5. Select partners. B goes on stage and waits for A to enter. A decides upon a definite character relationship with B, but does not tell B. B must discover who she is by the way A relates and talks with her. B must play the

scene throughout, responding as best she can until he discovers who she is. Then continue playing the scene until the teacher calls "curtain." Suggestions:

A is a teenager coming home late; B is the mother.

A is a clerk in an antique shop who has broken an expensive bowl; B is the manager.

6. Show character and situation through door knocking only. If possible, students participating should stand outside the classroom door and knock without being seen by the class. Examples:

Knock as a police officer at night, demanding door to be opened

A very young child unable to reach door knob

A gangster entering a hideaway

A delivery boy with a telegram

7. Indicate character and situation through use of your legs and feet only. Have two classmates hold a covering in front of your torso and head, showing only your legs and feet. Create a character and a situation.

8. Indicate character and situation through your hands only by having them show from a partition in a curtain.

Adapted from Fran Tanner, *Basic Drama Projects*, 5th ed., pp. 25–26 (Caldwell, ID: Clark Publishing, 1987). Used by permission.

• •

A PICTURE AND A THOUSAND WORDS

Grade Level: K–3

    Objective: To learn a simple story from pictures

    Procedure: Use wordless picture books—books which have illustrations, but no words—to stimulate storytelling. Students tell the story using their own words. Not all wordless picture books tell a story, so careful choice is important. Some of my favorites are:

Good Dog, Carl. Alexandra Day. La Jolla, CA: Green Tiger Press, 1985.

The Story of a Little Mouse Trapped in a Book. Monique Felix. La Jolla, CA: Green Tiger Press, 1980. (Also *The Further Adventures of the Little Mouse Trapped in a Book,* 1983.)

A Boy, a Dog, and a Frog. Mercer Mayer. New York: Dial Press, 1967. (Also *Frog, Where Are You?*, 1969; *Frog on His Own,* 1973.)

Two More Moral Tales. Mercer Mayer. New York: Four Winds Press, 1974.

The Surprise Picnic. John Goodall. New York: Atheneum, 1977. (Also *Shrewbettina's Birthday.* San Diego: Harcourt Brace Jovanovich, 1970.)

Changes, Changes. Pat Hutchins. New York: Macmillan, 1971.

Do You Want to Be My Friend? Eric Carle. New York: Thomas Crowell, 1971.

The Wrong Side of the Bed. Edward Ardizonne. Garden City, NY: Doubleday, 1970.

Goodnight, Dear Monster. Terry Nell Morris. New York: Random House, 1980.

Although not wordless, the *Mysteries of Harris Burdick* by Chris Van Allsburg (Boston: Houghton Mifflin, 1984) is great for story starters. The book consists of a series of drawings, each accompanied by a title and a caption that the reader can use to make up her own story.

. . . .

GROUP STORYTELLING

Grade Level: 3–12

Objective: To learn to tell a story

Materials Needed: Four short fables. [I use four from Arnold Lobel's award-winning book, *Fables* (New York: Harper and Row, 1980].

Procedure: Use the following steps to lead this activity.

1. Divide students into groups of four. Assign each group a fable. Have students read the fable silently. Have the groups discuss their initial impressions of the fable. Then have them read it aloud, round-robin style (each member having a turn to read). Ask students to discuss what they learned about the story after they read it aloud.

2. Have them read the story aloud again, with no student reading the same passage aloud that he did previously. Have group members discuss: If you were a picture book artist, which moments of the story would you choose to illustrate? Why? Describe the illustrations in detail.

3. Have students turn the text over and try a group telling, taking turns just as they did when they were reading. After the groups have finished, have them look back at the text and discuss: What was left out? What additions did you make that bring the story to life? How is the story growing in the oral tradition? (Most groups discover at this point that it is a good idea to memorize Lobel's morals just as he phrased them. This will be the only memorized part of the story; the rest will flow naturally from the student's knowledge of the story.)

4. Have students try a second group telling. Have them stand for this telling.

5. Finally, have each student "tell to the wall," literally. Each student should move to the wall and tell the story. This time is used for an out loud, dress rehearsal of the telling. Recombine the students into new groups of four so no teller is with a member of his previous group. Each group member now tells her fable. Have students share with one another the strengths of each student's telling.

• •

YOU'RE NOT ALONE

Grade Level: 3–12

   Objective: To learn a story collaboratively

Procedure: Tell students that learning a story need not be a solitary activity. One of the most effective ways to learn a story is to read it aloud to an audience. Have each student select a story to read. Divide students into small groups. After each student has read his story, the group members should rotate so that each student reads his story to every other student in the class. Then each student should return to her original group and tell the story, without the aid of the text.

• •

GROUP STORY DEVELOPMENT

Grade Level: 3–12

   Objective: To "play" with the elements of delivery and with translation of written material into oral form

Procedure: Use the following steps to lead this activity.

1. Divide the class into five small groups. Assign each group the task of developing a different element for story delivery for the same story.

> *Group 1:* characterization through voice
>
> *Group 2:* characterization through posturing
>
> *Group 3:* visual imagery through body movement
>
> *Group 4:* interpretation through pitch and phrasing
>
> *Group 5:* audience participation through various means

2. When each group has completed its task, reassign group memberships so that one member of the original five groups is now in each of the five new groups. Each of the new groups will thus have access to all of the techniques invented by the first five groups. Each group member presents the decisions about elements of delivery as discussed in the first grouping. One member of each second group, finally, is chosen to integrate all of the interpretive information into a full storytelling. Allow a week for these individuals to "work out" their respective deliveries; then have them present all five versions of the same story to the entire class.

3. Divide the class into several smaller groups. Give each group two stories, one that is the same and another that is different from those given to the other groups. Each group will read the stories. (Multiple copies that can be read out of class will save time.) Each group must develop a form of direct audience participation for each of the two stories, and then devise a means of teaching the audience its part or bringing the audience "in."

Each group then chooses two individuals to tell the two stories for the entire group, using the participation inventions.

Note: Such group activity serves at least two purposes: (1) It allows novice tellers to solve encoding problems collectively, to create, invent, and design interpretive elements as a community, and (2) it brings the nature and process of solving encoding problems to the conscious attention of the tellers.

From Norma Livo and Sandra Rietz, *Storytelling Activities,* p. 51 (Littleton, CO: Libraries Unlimited, 1987). Used by permission.

DELIVERY PRACTICE SEQUENCE

Grade Level: 7–12
  Objective: To concentrate on aspects of story delivery
  Procedure: Have students tell the same story using the following procedure.

For the Very First Telling: Have each storyteller practice controlling for tense, for linguistic "garbage" (mazes and false starts), for interpretation of characters through voice, for pitch, and for phrasing—essentially all linguistic elements. The teller may sit or stand for story delivery. There is little concern at this point with what the body does; for example, the hands are free to do or not do what they will. The first story may be delivered while sitting.

For the Second Telling: Have each storyteller pay attention to the body, to facial expression, and to posturing, movement, and extension. While the attitude of the body should be natural throughout telling, the teller is now becoming aware of the potential of the body for delivering visual imagery. The teller learns, here, to control for paralinguistic devices, while still incorporating all of the elements that applied to the first telling. The second story must be told while standing.

For the Third Telling: Have each storyteller develop audience interaction for a chosen story. Then have the teller devise a way of introducing the interaction to the audience or otherwise drawing the audience into the play. The teller must also retain, where appropriate, all of the linguistic and paralinguistic elements that applied to the first two tellings.

For the Fourth Telling: Have each storyteller develop a prop for the telling of the story. Add the prop to all the techniques utilized for the first three tellings (audience interaction optional). The prop must be an integral part of the telling, a part of the story. It must not "take over" the story, but its purpose must also be clear.

Between each of the above tellings, introduce the students to technique and allow for opportunity both to practice and to hear other storytellers. The four tellings are spaced at two-week intervals.

Adapted from Norma Livo and Sandra Rietz, *Storytelling Activities,* p. 52 (Littleton, CO: Libraries Unlimited, 1987). Used by permission.

PREPARATION IS THE BEGINNING

Grade Level: 3–12
Objective: To prepare a story for telling
Materials Needed: Preparation Forms 1, 2, 3
Procedure: Have students complete the preparation forms. These could become a part of their storytelling journals.

PREPARATION FORM 1: PLOT OUTLINE

Name ....

Write the major steps in the action of your story.

PREPARATION FORM 2: STORY ANALYSIS

Name ....

Title of my story ....

Author ....

Audience for which this story is appropriate ....

This is appropriate for this audience because:

Plot Summary:

PREPARATION FORM 3: CHARACTER ANALYSIS

Name ....

Build your own mental picture of each of the characters in your story. Complete this form for each character:

Character's name ....

Age ....   Sex ....

Describe the character's voice:

Describe the character's physical appearance (posture, gestures, dress):

Describe the typical language the character would use (phrases, slang, etc.):

Character's educational level ....

Occupation ....

Any other pertinent information:

• •

INTRODUCTION PLEASE

Grade Level: 3–12
Objective: To create an introduction for your story
Materials Needed: Introduction Form
Procedure: Have each student write an introduction for a story using the Introduction Form.

INTRODUCTION FORM

Name ....

Attention getter:

Creating the setting (time and place):

Explain why you chose to tell this story:

STORY YARN

Grade Level: All

Objective: To introduce story sequencing

Materials Needed: A long piece of yarn with unevenly spaced knots tied in it. The yarn is rolled into a ball.

Procedure: Have students sit in a circle. Have the student starting the story hang on to the end of the yarn and unravel the yarn as he tells the story. The teller of the story changes whenever the teller gets to a knot; the teller then gives the yarn to the person next to him and that person continues the story.

STORY MAPPING

Grade Level: All

Objective: To learn story sequence and plot structure

Procedure: Have students choose a story and draw all parts of a story on one page. Tell them that stick figures are fine: this is not an art project. The idea is to get the main parts of the story illustrated so they can tell the story from their picture. I tell my students that when they go home at night and tell what happened to them during the day, they do not think in words, they think in pictures. Too often, students want to memorize a story word for word. They should visualize the story and tell the story from the visualization. Students can use arrows to show movement, numbering, plus or equal signs, circles, etc. Mapping is like taking notes on a lecture, except the notes of mapping are in picture form. Have students share their maps with other students.

CAULDRON OF STORY

Grade Level: K–6

Objective: To understand the motifs of storytelling

Materials Needed: Four containers to serve as cauldrons

Procedure: Use the following steps to lead this activity:

1. Tell students that J.R.R. Tolkien, author of *The Hobbit,* says that the cauldron of story has been boiling since the beginning of time. Into it are put all the tastiest bits of life: images of the terrible, the comic, the awesome, the littlest, the biggest, the high and the mighty, the low and

humble, and on and on and on. Folklorists would call these bits "motifs," or recurring images or patterns—for example, the witch, or the "happily ever after" ending.

2. To help students create their types of folktales, find four containers that will serve as cauldrons. Explain the recurrence of certain types of motifs in folktales, as above. Also discuss the ingredients for a good story.

3. Then have four categories written on the board—characters, events, objects, and settings—explaining that these are the four major categories of motifs found in folktales. Brainstorming with students, begin writing examples under each of the categories until a long list of each of the four is arrived at.

4. Then have students write each of the words or phrases on the board on a slip of paper. Put these into the appropriate cauldron. Mix well. Have each student or a representative from a group take a slip of paper from each cauldron and create a story. Share the results, saving time for student observations and comments.

Adapted from Sheila Dailey, *Storytelling: A Creative Teaching Strategy.* Copyright © 1985 by Storytime Productions, Mt. Pleasant, MI. Used by permission.

TELL ME WHY

Grade Level: All
Objective: To create "why" stories
Procedure: Read several stories from Rudyard Kipling's *Just So Stories.* Have students create their own "why" stories and tell them to one another.

STORYTELLING CINQUAIN

Grade Level: 3–6
Objective: To understand the importance of picture words in stories
Materials Needed: Large sheet of paper; small, colorful scraps of paper
Procedure: Having heard several tales, very likely students are full of the sights and sounds of story. Have students write a folktale cinquain (a five-line poem) by first picking a character in one of the folktales they remember and then writing it according to the following pattern:

Line One: one word (a noun)
Line Two: two words (adjectives)
Line Three: three words (verbs)

Line Four: four words (show feelings or teller's relationship to the noun in line one)

Line Five: one word (a synonym for the word used in line one)

Example:

Girl
Sweet, lovely
Scrubbed, cleaned, cried
Danced away her tears
Cinderella

Discuss with students the importance of picture words in stories (concrete words that paint a picture in the imagination). Have them close their eyes and picture a character in a story they have just heard. Is the character tall or short, fat or thin, happy or sad? What color are the character's clothes?

What sort of house does the character live in? After answering questions such as these, have students draw an outline of the character on a large sheet of paper and tape it up so all can see, write the words the students used to describe the character on small, colorful scraps of paper, and paste the words in an array around the character outline.

Adapted from Nancy Polette, *Activities with Folktales and Fairy Tales.* Copyright © 1979, Book Lures, Inc., O'Fallon, MO. Reprinted with permission.

• •

THE LORE OF YOUR FOLK

Grade Level: 7–12

Objective: To understand that folklore is still part of our society

Procedure: Share the excerpt below with students. Then ask them to find out the folklore of their school and community. They could then develop the folklore into story form and tell the stories.

Bearers of folk tradition live in mountain cabins, yes, but in tenements, split-levels, and high-rises as well. The folk are all of us. And folklore plays a vital but unappreciated role in holding together the frayed, factory-made fabric of our lives. Whether it be useful or silly, true or false, folklore connects us to the past and to each other, because it requires face-to-face contact. It exists when people share an identity, when they recognize themselves as members of a group united by race, nationality, occupation, class, geography, or age; and since all of us once belonged to that group of human beings we call children, the folklore of childhood brings together all of us.

Mary and Herbert Knapp, *One Potato, Two Potato: The Secret Education of American Children,* p. 3. Copyright © 1976, W. W. Norton and Company, Inc., New York. Used by permission.

. . . .

STORYTELLING CORNER

Grade Level: K–3

Objective: To provide a classroom space where students can tell stories

Procedure: Establish a storytelling corner in the classroom. Equip this area with a variety of props that may be used to stimulate story building and sharing. Include a tape recorder so students can tape their stories so others can listen to them. Make the corner inviting with rugs, pillows, plants, etc.

. . . .

STORYTELLING JOURNAL

Grade Level: 7–12

Objective: To keep a written record of stories heard or learned

Procedure: Inform the students that this journal is a place for each of them to keep a record of the stories they hear, a list of stories they might like to tell, newspaper articles that might be good for telling, and so on.

. . . .

MOOD MUSIC

Grade Level: All

Objective: To create a mood

Procedure: Have students listen to an instrumental musical selection and ask them to tell a story based on the mood set by the music.

. . . .

THE VISITOR

Grade Level: All

Objective: To hear professional storytellers

Procedure: Ask your librarian for names of professional storytellers in your community. Invite one or more to class to tell stories and to talk about the art of storytelling.

Option: One of your students might have a parent or grandparent who is a good storyteller and would enjoy coming to your class to tell stories.

STORYTELLING TROUPE

Grade Level: 7–12

Objective: To form a storytelling troupe that takes stories to various places in the community

Procedure: Help students form a storytelling troupe. They will have to choose their stories, preferably around a theme. They might also design a T-shirt to wear when they perform. They should be primarily responsible for making the arrangements to tell the stories. Stories could be told at nursing homes, retirement homes, church groups, elementary school classrooms, hospitals.

QUILTING BEE

Grade Level: 3–12

Objective: To build a sense of community

Procedure: Explain to students the idea of a quilting bee. In pioneer days women would gather to make quilts. But perhaps as important as the quilt was the chance to visit with one another—to gossip, to tell stories, to talk over problems. In terms of our present day, you also could explain about the AIDS Quilt and how it has been a way of healing sorrow for many people. Following these discussions, have students make a quilt of their classroom or their school or their community. Each student should make a block. The blocks can be actual cloth, later sewn together, or paper taped together. Each quilt should represent a story the student wants to tell about his class, school, or community.

• •

TOY INTERVIEW

Grade Level: 3–12

Objective: To conduct an interview and use the information to create a story

Materials Needed: Interview Form

Procedure: Have students interview a grandparent, a parent, an aunt, an uncle, a cousin, or an older brother or sister about their favorite toy. Students can use the Interview Form included here or make up their own. After completing the interview, students are to make up a story about the toy and tell it to classmates.

INTERVIEW FORM

Person Interviewed:

1. Name and describe the toy or game that was your favorite when you were my age:

2. Why was it your favorite?

3. Where did you buy toys?

4. Which toys and games of your childhood are still sold today?

· ·

FAMILY FOLKLORE

Grade Level: All

Objective: To collect family stories and tell them

Materials Needed: Family Folklore Interview Form

Procedure: Have students collect family folklore. They might research their ancestry, origins of family names, and traditions. Students can interview family members using the Family Folklore Interview Form. After gathering family folklore, each student might want to make a copy of the folklore for other family members or tell the stories to other family members.

FAMILY FOLKLORE INTERVIEW FORM

Person interviewed: ....

Family relationship: ....

Place of birth: ....   Year of birth: ....

Profession: ....

Where did you grow up? ....

What is your fondest childhood memory? ....

....

....

....

When you were growing up, did you have any pets? ....

....

What did you do for fun? ....

....

What was your school like? ....

Who was your favorite teacher? ....   Why? ....

What was the most important turning point in your life—a time when you might have gone a different direction? What happened? ....

....

....

What were your father's parents like? ....

....

Your mother's parents? ....

....

Can you remember any stories they told you? ....

....

What was the hardest work you ever did? ....

....

Do you have any special family traditions? ....

....

What was your favorite Christmas (Thanksgiving, Fourth of July, Halloween)? Why? What happened? ....

....

Did you ever do anything for which you had to be punished? ....

....

What would you still like to accomplish in your lifetime? ....

....

What is your most prized possession? ....

Why? ....

....

Interviewer: Write down your impression of the person you interviewed. Also write down your favorite memory of this person. Write any additional notes, or draw a sketch of the person.

• •

TELL IT WITH PUPPETS

Grade Level: All
  Objective: To use puppets in storytelling
  Procedure: Use puppets to tell many stories.

Puppets come in all shapes and sizes—finger puppets; sock puppets; hand puppets; marionettes; rod puppets; paper plate puppets; stick, box, paper bag, and tube puppets; wooden spoon puppets; clothespin puppets, and so on. To familiarize yourself with puppets and to guide your students in their interest in puppets, the following sources will be helpful.

Books on puppetry

Books on puppetry available from the Puppeteers of American Puppetry Store, P.O. Box 3128, Santa Ana, CA 92703:

Baird, Bill. *The Art of Puppetry*

Barchelder, Marjorie. *The Puppet Theatre Handbook*

Cochrane, Louise. *Shadow Puppets in Color*

Dowie, Fran, and Louise Glennie. *Big Is Beautiful*

Engler, Larry, and Carol Fljan. *Making Puppets Come Alive*

Flower, Cedric, and Alan Fortney. *Puppets—Methods and Materials*

Johnson, Janibeth. *Shadow Puppetry on the Overhead Projector*

Latshaw, George. *Puppetry—The Ultimate Disguise*

Lewis, Shari, and Lillian Oppenheimer. *Folding Paper Puppets*

Simmers, Rene. *The World of Puppets*

Wilt, Joy, and Gwen and John Hurn. *Puppets with Pizazz*

Additional resources

Bodor, John. *Creating and Presenting Hand Puppets*. New York: Reinhold Publishing, 1967.

Currell, David. *Puppetry for School Children*. Newton, MA: Charles T. Branford Co., 1970.

Gates, Frieda. *Easy-to-Make Puppets*. New York: Harvey House Publishers, 1976.

Hopper, Grizella. *Puppets Throughout the Grades*. Worcester, MA: Davis Publications, 1966.

Richter, Dorothy. *Fell's Guide to Hand Puppets*. New York: Frederick Fell, Inc., 1970.

Slade, Richard. *You Can Make a String Puppet*. Boston: Plays Inc., 1966.

Van Gilder, Amy. *Felt Toy Making: Advanced Techniques.* New York: Drake Publishers, Inc., 1974.

Williams, DeAtna. *Paper-Bag Puppets.* Belmont, CA: Fearon Publishers, 1966.

Williams, DeAtna. *More Paper-Bag Puppets.* Belmont, CA: Fearon Publishers, 1966.

Worrell, Estelle Ansley. *Be a Puppeteer!* New York: McGraw-Hill, 1969.

OVERHEAD SHADOW PUPPET

Grade Level: 3–6

Objective: To use puppets in storytelling

Materials Needed: Light tagboard, manila file folders or other stiff paper, drinking straws, clear and colored acetate (book report covers), permanent marker pens, double-stick scotch tape, paper fastener brads, yarn, and thread

Procedure: Have students choose a simple story to tell. Generally a folktale with only a few characters is best. Help students use the following instructions to make an overhead shadow puppet. Each student should tell his story using the shadow puppets he has made.

How to make an overhead shadow puppet

1. Cut out image from paper. Cut decorating slits or other features with thread scissors or hole punch. Attach a straw rod control or acetate strip to back of puppet using one of the following methods:

   Method A: Using drinking straw, wrap a piece of masking tape around end of straw. Let tape extend at the end of straw ½ inch, and attach tape extension to back of puppet with another piece of tape.

   Method B: Using clear acetate strip, lay tip of strip flat on back of puppet and adhere with double-stick tape. Add a piece of folded masking tape on end of acetate for hand grip.

2. For movable features, hinge body parts together by punching holes where joints meet and securing with a paper fastener. Attach straw, or acetate rod, controls to both body and moving parts sections for animating. To incorporate colored details on characters, cut out decorative holes in the basic puppet, such as spots on a leopard or eyes on a cat. Colored acetate can be overlaid on the holes with double-stick tape, resulting in a leopard with orange spots or a cat with green eyes. Yarn and thread can be used for whiskers and hair.

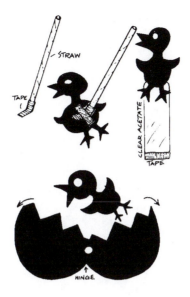

To Operate: Lay the puppet image flat on overhead glass with rod control bent to one side, away from path of light. Move the puppet along the glass surface using the perimeter of the glass as a frame of reference. When manipulating controls, keep hands as much to the side as possible to avoid blocking out the light source.

From Nancy Renfro and Nancy Frazier, *Imagination: At Play with Puppets and Creative Drama,* p. 51. Copyright © 1987 Nancy Renfro Studios, Inc., P.O. Box 164226, Austin, TX 78716, 1-800-933-5512. Used by permission.

SHADOW BOX THEATRE

Grade Level:	7–12
Objective:	To use shadow puppets to tell a story
Materials Needed:	Read the information on shadow puppets and shadow boxes by F. Rottman.
Procedure:	Have each student present a story using the shadow box technique. Shadow puppets are an ancient form of puppetry used by Chinese and other Asian cultures. When placed behind a shadow screen, using rear light projection, the resulting images create a dreamlike impression. Stories should have few characters and a simple sequential plot. Eric Carle's *The Mixed-Up Chameleon* (New York: Harper and Row, 1984) is an excellent example of a story that can be told effectively using a shadow box.

Shadow puppets

A shadow puppet is a cutout figure held by a rod, against a white screen and in front of a strong light (sketch A). As a result, the figure's silhouette appears on the front of the screen (sketch B).

These puppets may be very simple figures cut from black construction paper or an elaborate, colorful figure with articulated (moving) parts.

Shadow puppetry involves three elements: (1) a screen; (2) a strong light, such as a desk lamp; and (3) figures.

The first step is to make a screen. Then you can experiment using different kinds of figures or shapes on it.

Screen

Begin shadow puppetry with this very simple screen.

Materials: A cardboard box (approx. 15 × 21 inches—37.52 × 50 cm); a piece of white fabric (such as a discarded bed sheet) large enough to cover the bottom of box; a knife, stapler, yardstick, pencil, ruler, and scissors.

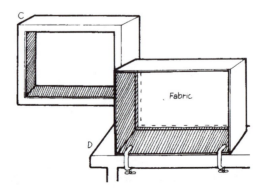

Procedure: Use knife to cut flaps off box. Cut an opening in bottom of box, leaving a 2-inch (5 cm) frame on each side (sketch C).

On the inside of box, cover opening with fabric. Staple in place. Fabric must be kept taut. Place screen on table. The screen has to be weighted or clamped to table so it will not tip over. Place several heavy books or a brick for weight in the box. Or clamp box to table with C clamps (sketch D).

Place bright light behind screen so it will shine on screen, but not show the shadow of puppeteers (sketch A).

Simple figures

Materials: Black construction paper, scissors, small paper fasteners, paper punch, two plastic drinking straws, masking tape.

Procedure: Enlarge a figure pattern (see "Patterns") and trace onto black construction paper. Cut out figure. The figure may be left in one piece or made with movable parts. To make an articulated (moving) figure, cut out separate pieces to make figures. On each piece include area indicated by broken lines (sketch E). Punch holes where indicated on pattern. Fasten figure pieces together with paper fasteners so pieces move freely.

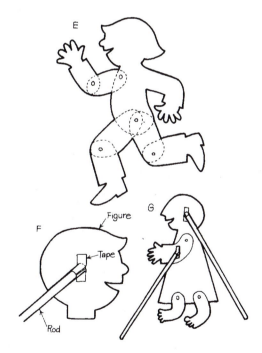

To attach rod (plastic straw) to figure, tape a piece of masking tape to each side of rod and to figure as shown in sketch F. This procedure allows rod to fold flat for storage. A rod has to be attached to each part the puppeteer wants to control. Feet are often left free to dangle (sketch G).

Use rods to hold figure close to screen, as shown in sketch A. Press figures against screen to avoid a ghosting effect.

Additional figures

To make figures other than those suggested, experiment drawing figures free-hand. Draw figure first on newspaper, then transfer figure to a more permanent material. It is important that each shadow puppet have a clear profile. Figures do not have to be accurately drawn, or be in correct proportion to each other. Or use figures from coloring and storybooks for patterns. Or look through your Sunday School curriculum visuals for appropriate figures. Use them for patterns; or attach a rod and use them as figures.

Shadow puppets can be made from materials and in colors other than black construction paper. Colored lightweight cardboard, aluminum foil, tracing paper or parchment paper may be used successfully. When using lightweight paper, strengthen the paper to withstand use. First, draw pattern onto the paper. Then use felt pens to add color. Place paper between two pieces of clear, self-adhesive vinyl. Color will show on the screen.

Additional ways to join figure pieces

Thread—Use a large needle to make holes in figure. Reinforce hold with cellophane tape. Cut a length of button/carpet thread and tie a large knot in one end. With a large-eye needle, insert thread through figure pieces where indicated. Pull thread until knot is against figure; remove needle and tie knot on the opposite side of figure (sketch H). Tie knot so pieces will move freely.

Wire—Bend a length of lightweight wire (approx. 28-gauge) into a T shape. Insert ends of wire through figure; open ends flat against figure (sketch I).

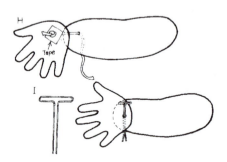

Additional control rods

Use ⅛-inch (.3 cm) dowel, 12 inches (30 cm) long. Or use wooden skewers (available from hardware stores). Attach to figure in similar manner as for straws. See sketches F and G. If puppeteer's hand shows on screen while manipulating figures, make rods longer.

Color and special effects

Although shadow puppets are traditionally black silhouettes, figures made from colored materials may also be used effectively. Or color white paper figures with felt pens.

To achieve a special effect, cut out parts of a figure so light shines through. Use an X-acto knife or manicure scissors to cut out the sections. Also, use a paper punch to punch out a design or figure (sketch J).

Cut slits for eyes, hair, costume, or other features. Slits or cutout sections may be covered with colored cellophane or tissue paper. Cutout sections can also be covered with small pieces of lace, nylon net, or paper doilies (sketch K).

If figure seems weakened by the cutout areas, cover both sides of figure with clear, self-adhesive vinyl so figure is sandwiched between the vinyl.

Scenery

Cut scenery outline from lightweight cardboard and place in front of screen or behind it. To make scenery stand, insert scenery outline in a piece of styrofoam (2 × 2 inches [5 × 5 cm] and the length of screen opening). Place styrofoam inside the box (sketch L).

Construction paper scenery can be taped directly to the inside of screen.

To make colored scenery, cut scenes from the tissue paper and glue to clear piece of plastic. Acetate or Mylor (available from art supply stores) may also be used. The more layers of tissue paper applied to plastic, the darker the color will appear. Vary the layers so some features will appear darker than others. The plastic pieces containing scenery can rest against the screen. When one play has several scenes, glue the scenery for each scene to different pieces of plastic. To change scene, turn off light and place next scene against screen.

Materials such as dried leaves, ferns, and weeds add interest to background scenes. Arrange these materials on the sticky side of a piece of clear, self-adhesive vinyl. Then place another piece of vinyl on top of materials so they are sandwiched between the two pieces of vinyl. Pieces of nylon net, lace, and paper doilies can also be used similarly for scenery.

Patterns

These patterns can be enlarged for use as shadow or rod puppets.

Enlarging a Pattern

1. Draw a grid of 1-inch (2.5 cm) squares onto paper.
2. Copy the design from pattern square by square onto your grid.

Shadow Puppets

Figures may be used as one piece or made with movable parts. To make a moving figure, cut out separate pieces to make figure. Include area indicated by broken lines. Punch holes where indicated on patterns. Fasten pieces together with one of the suggested fasteners.

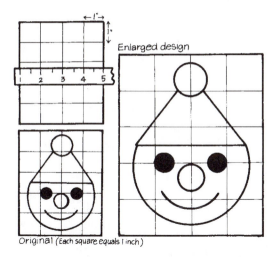

Rod Puppets

To use figures for rod puppets, cut pattern outline from lightweight cardboard. Add facial and clothing details with felt pens. Tape figures to an ice-cream stick or tongue depressor.

If a figure has to face the opposite direction, simply turn over pattern and trace onto paper or cardboard. Add facial and clothing details.

From F. Rottman, *Easy to Make Puppets and How to Use Them*, pp. 39–41. Copyright © 1985, Regal Books, Ventura, CA. Used by permission.

• •

INTERCULTURAL STORIES I

Grade Level: 7–12

Objective: To understand other cultures through storytelling

Procedure: Give students the instructions below to help them begin writing their own personal anecdotes. Have each student tell his own story aloud in class. Use these anecdotes as starting points for a discussion of intercultural communication. Discuss what the student learned about the other culture as well as his own. Also discuss what intercultural communication principles can be used to make sense of the stories.

"You will tell a story about an intercultural experience that happened to you. Each story will begin with the statement: I am a (age, nationality, and sex) and a (choose a relevant adjective such as hilarious, frightening, heartwarming, terrifying, confusing, infuriating, etc.) crosscultural incident that happened to me occurred in (place and date)."

Sample personal anecdote

I am a 46-year-old American woman living in Hong Kong, and a heartwarming intercultural incident that happened to me occurred on the MTR (subway) on September 21, 1993.

You need to know that I hate the MTR. It's too crowded. I never ceased to be amazed at the number of people who can squeeze into each car. Since I am American, I like my personal space. I don't like strangers standing right in my face or sitting or standing with their bodies smashed into mine. This makes me very uncomfortable. As a way to handle my discomfort, I read as I travel. That way I can ignore the closeness, pushing, and shoving.

On September 21, 1993, I was standing in a very crowded car. I was hanging on to a pole with one hand and holding my book in the other. Suddenly, I felt a light tap on my hand. I ignored it. A few seconds later I felt another tap. I ignored it. A few seconds later I felt yet another tap. This time I did not ignore it! I was angry! I jerked my head up from my book, put a most disgusted expression on my face, and looked down in the direction from whence the tap came.

I stared into the face of a very old, very wizened Chinese man who was sitting next to where I was standing. He began talking to me in Cantonese and rose, indicating with his gestures that I should take his seat.

I replied, "No, no. That's OK. You keep your seat." In my culture it would be rude to take his seat. After all, he was much older and more frail than I. I could plant my feet and not fall when the train swayed or people pushed and shoved to get on or off the train. He looked frail enough to be "sent flying" with the smallest provocation.

He continued to insist. I continued to decline. Finally, a young Chinese man tapped me on the shoulder and said in English, "Please take his seat. It will do him great honor. He wants you to have it because he sees by the folder you carry that you are a professor at the Chinese University." (My purple folder, with "Chinese University of Hong Kong" in bold gold letters, and my name, "Professor Pamela Cooper," in not as bold black letters, had given away my identity.)

I nodded, said "Mm goy" (thank you), and sat down. He stood, swaying with the train's movements and being nearly knocked over several times by the frenzied crowd, for five more stops. When he left the train, he turned to wave at me.

Whenever I ride the MTR, with all my frustration at its rudeness and lack of breathing space, and lack of even a small ounce of the milk of human kindness, I remember that old man and smile.

INTERCULTURAL STORIES II

Grade Level: 7–12
  Objective: To understand other cultures through storytelling
  Procedure: The following activities can help students understand
       other cultures.

A. Each student tells a myth, legend, or folktale from a specific culture. These are presented to the class. The discussion that follows centers on (1) the student's performance, and (2) the cultural value communicated by the story.
B. Each student writes and then tells a fable. Discussion focuses on the cultural value communicated in the fable and the effect this value has on communication with others.
C. Have students read the book *Mai Pen Rai Means Never Mind,* by Carol Hollinger (1993). This is a story of an American woman's experience living in Thailand. Next, students read a children's book by Emily Cheney Neville, *The China Year* (1991), which is a story of a young American girl's experience living in China. For comparison, then read *In the Year of the Boar and Jackie Robinson* (Lord, 1984), the story of a young Chinese girl who moves to America. Using the experiences they read about in the books, students create their own stories. For example, take a character in one of the books and tell a story about her ten years after the book's story ends.

THE "KAMISHIBAI"

Grade Level: 3–6
  Objective: To understand that every culture has stories and storytellers
  Procedure: Follow the steps below.

1. Explain the following to the students: The kamishibai (kah-mee-shee-bye), a paper theatre in a box, is a Japanese version of "moving pictures." It is a storytelling device that can be used in any country. In Japan, the story man with his kamishibai mounted on the rear of his bicycle rides along until he comes to a group of children. Leaving his bicycle, he walks among the children, gaining their attention by clapping together two wooden blocks, ringing a small bell, or sounding notes on a flute.

   The Japanese children, anticipating the story, happily follow the man and take their places in front of his paper theater. With a flourish, the story man opens the kamishibai, which becomes the stage, and fits into place a whole set of bright picture cards. On the first one is printed the story's title, on all the others are painted the story's brightly colored illustrations. The words of the story appear on the backs of the pictures so they can be read aloud. The story that accompanies a picture appears on the back of the preceding picture.

When the children are quiet, the story man begins to tell his story and with changing voice and appropriate gestures, continues to the climax, when he stops, stretches out his hand, and waits to receive coins from the listeners. Then, satisfied with his payment, he completes his story.

2. Have students make a kamishibai. The box may be almost any kind, from a carton, plain and undecorated, to a made-for-the-purpose wooden box with gaily painted curlicues of gilt, a border of crimson, and a decorated cloth curtain to pull across the "stage" opening at the beginning and end of the performance.

3. To make the theater, cut an opening in the front of the box to allow a two- or three-inch frame around the opening. Do the same across the back of the box, and cut a long, narrow slit across the top of the box. The pictured illustrations are made on identical size paper and are viewed through the box's opening as the story unfolds. Each picture remains separate, and the complete set, arranged in sequence, is slipped down into the box through the narrow slit at the top.

As each picture is viewed, it is lifted from its place by the story person and replaced at the back of the set so, at the completion of the story, the pictures are in order for the next telling.

4. One student may be the story person and walk among the class, calling them to attention in Japanese fashion with the clap-clap of wooden blocks. Then, taking her place beside the kamishibai paper theater, she shows each picture in turn while other students enact the story's scenes through dialogue and gesture.

Adapted from *Let's Play a Story*, by Elizabeth Allstrom. Copyright © 1957 by Friendship Press, Inc. Used by permission.

· ·

TELL IT WITH A FLANNEL BOARD

Grade Level: 3–6
Objective: To tell a story using a flannel board
Materials Needed: Read the information by Jean Stangl on flannel boards.
Procedure: Have students choose a simple story—one with few characters and a simple, sequential plot. Have each student tell his story using a flannel board. Have students discuss the pros and cons of using this technique.

Introduction

A flannel graph is a board covered with felt or flannel, on which cutouts representing characters or objects are placed. It is a useful and important visual aid for presenting information, telling stories, and clarifying concepts.

Flannel graphs stimulate the imagination and attract and hold the attention of children. Most children learn through visual stimulation, and flannel graphs help them retain more information. The added tactile experience of the cutouts provides an additional sensory dimension. Auditory skills, sequencing skills, and oral language skills are also improved through flannel graph presentations.

Children will develop verbal language skills by participating in group stories and rhymes, and they will develop math readiness skills through exercises in grouping and counting. Having children place the figures on the board at the appropriate time allows for individual involvement.

For the teacher, the flannel graph can also be a valuable tool for introducing concepts of health, safety, and nutrition. For the student, it becomes a pathway for creating, discovering, and reinforcing. By placing figures on the felt board, the young child develops eye-hand coordination. Participating in adding and removing colorful figures will improve short attention spans. Through this involvement, both the restless child and the withdrawn child will be better able to cope with their behavior problems. Children can overcome self-consciousness while using the flannel graphs and figures for self-expression. Seeing the story sequence can aid the disorganized child, and the uncooperative child will discover flannel graphs to be a cooperative activity. The self-centered child will come to know the pleasure of sharing.

Older students can construct their own characters and develop short oral stories, make lesson presentations, and devise games.

Flannel graphs require extra time to prepare, as well as a certain amount of practice in order to be used as effective visual aids. They do, however, provide the novice presenter (adult or child) with the added security of a tangible prop while working before an audience.

How to make felt boards

Use any of the following materials for a base: Masonite, plywood, Celotex, bristol board, corrugated cardboard, cork, artists' portfolio, or boards from fabric bolts.

Felt boards, for use with a group, should be approximately two feet by three feet. They can be any shape, but rectangular boards are easier to use and store. A twelve-inch square makes a good lap board for use by either teacher or child. Larger boards can be hinged and folded for easier handling and storage.

A cigar box makes an excellent self-contained flannel graph kit. The outside of the box can be covered or painted and the figures kept in the box. Cover the inside of the lid with felt.

Cover boards with felt or heavy flannel. Yellow, beige, light blue, and black are the most popular colors. In cutting the felt, allow for a two-inch overlap on all sides. Stretch the felt tightly over the board. Secure it to the back side with staples or heavy tape. Do not glue the felt to the board because this weakens the static electricity that is needed to make the figures adhere. The board can also be covered with squares of indoor-outdoor carpet.

For an impromptu board, drape a piece of felt over a painting easel and secure it with several snap clothespins.

Set the finished board on a painting easel, chalk tray, or stand. You can make a satisfactory stand by screwing two large coat hooks into a piece of board twelve inches by three inches by one inch. Various types of easels can also be purchased at art supply stores. For best results, the board should rest at a slight slant.

Constructing figures

Select stories that have a few simple figures and repetitive themes. Don't make figures for all the characters or objects. Leave room for the imagination. Detailed backgrounds are hard to work with and are often distracting. However, at times, you may want to add an extra piece of felt for a mountain, sky, or ocean.

Figures can be constructed from felt, interfacing (Pelon), construction paper, or any other material that will adhere to the board. Construction paper figures can be laminated to make them sturdier and to prevent the colors from fading. Figures can be cut from old picture books and from magazines and catalogs. Lightweight paper should be reinforced. Add pieces of felt or sandpaper to the back of paper figures so that they will adhere to the board. Coloring books are a good source for simple patterns. Trace the pattern onto paper and then transfer it to felt. The pattern can be placed directly under Pelon and then traced.

If you wish to enlarge any pattern, use an opaque projector to do so. Simply trace the projected enlargement onto an appropriate material.

Tools for decorating

Felt pens, India ink, colored pencils, crayons, oil paints, and water paints can be used to decorate the figures. After decorating Pelon or felt with crayons or felt pens, place the figures between two sheets of wax paper and press with a warm iron. This will set the colors.

The most attractive and eye-catching patterns are those that are built up, as in a little boy with boots, mittens, coat, and hat. To make this pattern, first trace and cut out the figure of a boy. Then trace and cut out the boots, mittens, coat, and hat separately. Glue these to the basic figure. You may also cut out the facial features separately. If you use Pelon for the shapes, you can use pieces of felt for decoration.

Super Tacky glue is best for gluing felt. For best results, apply in a dot-to-dot fashion along the edges only. This glue also works well with Pelon.

Always make two sets of figures—one for yourself and one for the children. Children should have the opportunity to work with the figures and to reenact the story or activity. If pieces get lost or torn, you will always have the extra set.

Storage

Large manila envelopes make convenient storage places for the cutouts for individual flannel graphs. Fasten a copy of the story to a piece of tagboard or construction paper, and slip it in the envelope. Write the title at the top front, and file the envelope upright in a box. For the children's use, make a paper cutout depicting the contents of the envelope. Paste this to the top front of the envelope. Cover the storage box with colorful, adhesive-backed paper or wallpaper.

Flat boxes that can be stacked are also useful. They should be large enough so the figures can lie flat without being folded.

Self-locking plastic bags are another means for storing figures. Punch a hole in the top of the bag and hang it on a hook or a pegboard. Do not let small children play with plastic bags.

Presentation techniques

With practice and adequate preparation, the art of presenting flannel graph stories can soon be mastered. The following checklist will aid you in your presentation.

1. Know your story well. Flannel graph storytelling is a form of oral storytelling, so do not simply read the story. Poems and stories should be memorized.

2. Have your figures arranged in proper sequence so they can be placed on the board quickly and smoothly. Figures can be numbered on the back and placed in order upside down.

3. Place the board where all the children can see it. Do not have it so far from the children that they must strain their eyes or necks in order to see. Place it at a slant and as near the children's eye level as possible. Sit at the same level as the board.

4. After placing a figure on the board, press it firmly with your fingertips.

5. Add figures as they are mentioned. Keep the other figures out of sight, either behind the board or concealed in your lap. Remove all unnecessary figures so the board won't be cluttered and confusing.

6. Keep your eyes on the children, not on the board. Talk to the children, not to the board. This allows you to observe the children's reactions, expressions, and behavior. You will soon be aware of when to speed up, slow down, or repeat information.

7. Encourage children to participate by repeating words, phrases, or actions. Children can add or remove figures when appropriate, if it doesn't detract from the story.

8. If a child is restless or inattentive, try a little trick to recapture interest. Say, for example, "The little girl had brown hair and brown shoes—just like Joannie's" or "Brent, would you please hold the little elf until he is ready to go on the board?"
9. Practice your presentation before doing it for the children.

From *Flannelgraphs* by Jean Stangl. Copyright © 1986 by Fearon Teacher Aids, an imprint of Modern Curriculum, Simon & Schuster Elementary. Used by permission.

● ●

STORY GLOVES

Grade Level:	3–6
Objective:	To tell a story using a story glove
Materials Needed:	"Story Gloves" by Renfro and Hunt, below
Procedure:	Have each student choose a simple story. Have each student create a story glove for her story and tell the story using the story glove. Story gloves complement finger plays. Almost all gloves work well, and interchangeability can be achieved with a basic glove.

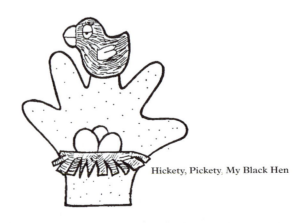

Hickety, Pickety, My Black Hen

Rubber household glove

This provides a smooth surface for adhering small picture images such as drawings, photographs, greeting cards, or magazine pictures. Cut out image and laminate with clear contact paper or plastic laminate for permanency, if desired. Put a piece of double-stick tape on the back of each image and secure to tips of glove.

Hickory, Dickory Dock   There was an Old Woman

Garden glove

Garden gloves come in an interesting variety of designs and colors while making a sturdy glove for all-around use. Sew small pieces of Velcro to tips of glove. Make characters from drapery pom-poms and glue corresponding pieces of Velcro to the backs of pom-poms for attaching to glove. Changing felt scenery such as a clock, moon, or palace can be attached to the palm area of glove by means of Velcro or a button.

Pelon glove

Make basic glove from heavyweight Pelon (interlining fabric). Use marker pens to color a scenic background, such as a garden, mountain, pond, or starlit sky. Paper images can be attached to the glove tips by means of paper clips. Open up the paper clip slightly, and glue or tape to back of image. Cut a crosswise slit on each glove tip about ⅓ inch down to insert the paper clip through.

From Nancy Renfro and Tamara Hunt, *Pocketful of Puppets: Mother Goose*, p. 16. Copyright © 1982, Nancy Renfro Studios, Inc., P.O. Box 164226, Austin, TX 78716, 1-800-933-5512. Used by permission.

• •

LET'S SAY IT TOGETHER

Grade Level: 3–12

Objective: To prepare and present a choral speaking presentation

Procedure: Good literature for choral speaking has three characteristics: strong rhythm, variety in mood, and a strong theme. Have students choose a poem with these characteristics and perform it in a choral speaking presentation. (A good source on choral speaking is "Group Interpretation," in K. Galvin, P. Cooper, and J. Gordon, *The Basics of Speech.* [Lincolnwood, IL: National Textbook Company, 1988], pp. 374–395.)

• •

CRITIQUING STORYTELLING

Grade Level: All (although forms are not appropriate for every level)

Objective: To enhance storytelling skills through critiquing the performances of others as well as our own

Procedure: Using any of the following forms, have students critique the storytelling performances of their classmates and their own performances. You will no doubt have to discuss the concept of critiquing as a means of improving storytelling skills. Students need to understand that critiques should include both the positive and negative aspects of the performance. In addition, students should be specific rather than general in their comments. When a negative comment is made, it should be followed by a suggestion as to what the teller might do in order to change the negative aspect into a positive one.

FORM 1

If possible, videotape each storyteller telling a story. Classmates and the teller can then critique and compare critiques using the following form:

The storyteller was (1) able to, (2) sometimes able to, (3) not able to:

motivate the audience to listen ....

convey action vividly ....

convey sequences of events clearly ....

assume character's point of view ....

express human motives ....

express human conflict ....

express human values ....

establish mood ....

use figurative speech ....

use language rhythmically ....

speak clearly and distinctly ....

utilize varied intonation ....

utilize appropriate gestures ....

utilize eye contact effectively ....

end the story gracefully ....

Form 1 adapted from Norma Livo and Sandra Rietz, *Storytelling Activities*, pp. 121–122. (Littleton, CO: Libraries Unlimited). Used by permission of Norma Livo.

FORM 2

Storyteller's Name .... Date ....

Title .... Author ....

Comments on:

1. Introduction (Was mood set? Was place set? Was time set? Were characters clear?)

2. Story (Was it appropriate? Did it seem believable? Was story concise, tight, held together? Was it fresh, new, entertaining? Was the story well told in terms of use of language, use of body and gestures, use of voice?)

3. Additional Comments:

Evaluator's Name ....

FORM 3

Rate each category using ratings of S for Superior, E for Excellent, G for Good, and F for Fair

Storyteller's Name ....

Choice of selection:

Was the selection told to a definite age group? ....

Voice and diction:

Was the voice quality, tone, pitch, rate, and range motivated by the moods of the selection? Was the technique smooth so that it did not call attention to itself? Was pronunciation accurate and acceptable? Was the volume right for the room? The selection? ....

....

....

Bodily action:

Did teller use appropriate gestures for the character? Was there physical poise in posture and movement? Did teller avoid distracting mannerisms and other unmotivated activity? ....

....

....

Interpretation:

Did teller seem to have insight and understanding of the story? Did teller place characters and change smoothly from one to another? Was characterization good? Was interpretation of spirit and emotional coloring in keeping with the mood of the selection? ....

....

....

Comments:

FORM 4

Storyteller's Name ....

1. Specifically, what did you like about this story?

2. How did the storyteller use language, voice, gesture, and body movement to help you create a mental image of the characters, setting, and time?

3. List five things you think the storyteller did that made the story enjoyable for you.

   a.

   b.

   c.

   d.

   e.

4. What suggestions for improvement would you make to this storyteller?

FORM 5

Circle the number (1=superior, 3=average, and 5=poor) that best represents your view of the storyteller's performance.

Selection:

1. Quality of material	1 2 3 4 5
2. Appropriate for storyteller, audience, occasion	1 2 3 4 5

Introductory remarks:

1. Established mood	1 2 3 4 5
2. Clarified unfamiliar words	1 2 3 4 5
3. Stimulated audience interest	1 2 3 4 5

Voice:

1. Pleasant quality	1 2 3 4 5
2. Flexible, expressive	1 2 3 4 5
3. Adequate volume	1 2 3 4 5
4. Appropriate words	1 2 3 4 5
5. Distinct enunciation	1 2 3 4 5
6. Grammatical accuracy	1 2 3 4 5

Presentation:

1. Logical development of ideas	1 2 3 4 5
2. Clear suggestion of character	1 2 3 4 5
3. Use of dialogue	1 2 3 4 5

Tempo:

1. Conveyed action and emotion	1 2 3 4 5
2. Built to a climax	1 2 3 4 5
3. Used pauses properly	1 2 3 4 5

Delivery:

1. Storyteller poised and relaxed	1 2 3 4 5
2. Bodily action coordinated with thought and emotion	1 2 3 4 5
3. Direct eye contact with audience	1 2 3 4 5
4. Conveyed enthusiasm	1 2 3 4 5

Additional suggestions:

Form 5 from Fran Tanner, *Basic Drama Projects,* 5th ed., pp. 25–26 (Caldwell, ID: Clark Publishing, 1987). Used by permission.

Meet the storyteller...
Kathy Phipps

Photo by Dawn Murray

Kathy Phipps is a teacher at Dawes School in Evanston, Illinois. She has formed an after-school Storytelling Club.

Q: Where did you get the idea for the Storytelling Club?

A: The Storytelling Club idea resulted from the death of my grandmother. Her death was extremely difficult for me, and I was having problems getting through the funeral service. When it was done, my grandmother's best friend (for over forty years) came up to me and said, "You know, I have a story about your grandmother that makes me remember and think of her." She told me a story about the first time she had seen my grandmother.

All these rumors had been flying about my grandmother and her first husband, who was divorced. They were moving and taking jobs with a large American corporation. My grandmother heard these rumors were flying about and decided if there were going to be rumors, she might as well give them something to have a rumor about. So the first day she got to her new home, she put on high-heels and a pair of shorts, grabbed a cigarette, put my mother in the baby carriage, and strolled down the block! Wearing high-heels, shorts, and with a cigarette! In those days, three of the most scandalous things a mother and wife could have done! So her soon-to-be best friend looked out her window and said, "That's a woman I've got to get to know!"

When I got back to my grandmother's house after the funeral, I looked through old family photo albums with my uncle, and he told me about the pictures I had not seen. I went home thinking about these pictures and regretting that I had not asked my grandmother about some of the stories "behind the pictures" before she had died. There was this one photograph that I found of her in a vaudeville show. And never in her life had she ever spoken of any artistic desires at all. She was a corporate secretary her entire life.

Q: But somewhere in this photograph there is a story...?

A: Yes. There's a story there and my uncle doesn't know it and my mother doesn't know it. It's gone. There is nobody who knows about this story. It is a lost story and it's one I really wish I could have known about because I think it's important when you begin to try to place yourself, when you start to form opinions about who you are in the frame of the people you come in contact with. I think it's important to have a sense of connectedness with other people. I know now that I'm not the only one who has this artistic urge. I'm not the only one in my family who had artistic leanings. I'm not this "thing" that came out of nowhere.

Q: So, the birth of the club really came from within you and your sense of lost stories?

A: Well, I have to give some credit to Lynn Rubright. The class I took from her helped me shape what was just a thought, what was really just an emotional response from me. Before Lynn's class, I didn't trust myself as a storyteller. She helped me with that. I began to have confidence that even if I was not a good storyteller, I could translate for kids. I could shape stories. If I couldn't come up with them myself, I at least had the ability to help others shape them.

Q: That's really important that people who don't necessarily perceive themselves as tellers can recognize themselves as having the ability to help others ...

A: I'm not a good storyteller. I make no pretense about that. And I tell that to my students.

Q: But I've heard you tell some wonderful stories. What do you say to your students when they say, "Ms. Phipps, I'm not a great storyteller?"

A: I say, "You don't have to be a great storyteller. You just have to be curious of what you feel inside." I tell them that storytelling is an incredibly personal art form, and it allows for as many different expressions as there are people. The only thing you really need is the confidence to access that material and some framing for that. And if you have someone who can teach you and develop enough confidence to access the material, then I really feel you can take that as far as you are personally willing to take it.

Q: What do you mean by "framing"?

A: Some of the stories you see the students tell as a first telling are very disorganized, not sequential, without thought to conversation, without thought to pacing. They come out as a first response to a story, which is how almost everyone tells a story based on an emotional experience. So then it takes either developing an objective eye or having someone objectify it for you—to go back and say, "Now you got it out.... What are the most crucial points of that story for you? What do you want to lead up to? What moment do you think you need to show as well as tell? Is there a point where conversation, where what they actually said, would help clarify that for us?"

Q: Do you help them structure?

A: Yes.

Q: Do you use questions?

A: I only use questions. It is rare for me to say, "Do this!" Frankly, at this point—no, actually from the beginning—after I have an initial talk about ways to do things and what to look for when you are shaping a story, I really defer to the kids. I say, "What are your suggestions for a second telling?"

I use a lot of peer evaluation. They have an understanding of what telling a story is like. I try very hard not to put in my impressions of a story, because that defeats the purpose of storytelling. Storytelling is a form you shape, from your understanding of the story.

Q: So you don't show them how to do it and say, "Now imitate me!"?

A: No, never.

Q: I'd like to talk a bit more about the Storytelling Club. Did you involve only students?

A: My concept was to include parents as a part of the club so that it would be a parent-student exchange. My invitation asked parents to be involved as well, to join us in our afternoon meetings, and that's also why I set up once-a-month evening performances. There were two purposes in that—one to give students performance experience. Also, I set up the evening performances so parents could come tell if they wanted to, and they could also share in the telling of their kids.

Q: So you initially wanted them to access family stories, but is that where you started?

A: No. Folktales is where I started, because they are easily accessible. They tend to have some dramatic moments in them, and many are humorous. It could have been too threatening, too personal to start with family stories. I did a whole school folklore unit. It was quite elaborate and would take forever to explain fully. So let me just say that every elementary student wrote an original folktale. I talked about the genre of folktales in classes, and the first story I told was a folktale. I invited Nancy Donoval to come to tell stories because one thing I wanted the students to get from the very beginning is that there is not one way to tell a story. I videotaped kids telling. I wanted them to be exposed to many different kids telling. The stories they told didn't have to be perfect. I've always admitted flaws to them. I tell students, "I'm a physical teller, but that's who I am as a person. I can't talk without using my body. But if you are a person who is not comfortable with that, you will still be a superior teller in your own way."

Q: And the club got started as a result of this unit?

A: The club got started after this unit and after the fifth graders did a family history unit and all the fifth graders told family stories. After that unit, I started the club. The unit was like sticking my foot into the water to see if it was warm, and it was! The response was incredible. Fifth graders would come running up to me in the hall and say, "Ms. Phipps, my dad told me the best story last night, and I can't wait to tell my story in drama." The kids were respectful listeners and responders because they understood that it was personal material.

Q: So the kids have responded very positively. What about the parents?

A: The parent reaction has been really excellent. One of the primary things has been their own increased involvement and enjoyment with their own family stories. At our last club performance night, I invited parents to tell. One parent told a story of something that happened to her, and then another parent said, "Yeah, you know ..." and this other story came pouring out. And then another father from across the room says, "Boy, that same kind of thing ..." and he told a story. And soon everyone was telling, and it started revolving around pets, so pet stories became the theme.

Q: How did the students feel about their parents' telling?

A: Kids jumped right in as soon as their parents were telling, and they'd say, "That's great, Mom, and do you remember ..." and they'd launch into something else. But Mom would say, "Yeah, but ..." and she would correct or add to it, and then Dad would jump in. It was this incredible dialogue going on. That kind of dialogue is missing in our culture. We don't have enough emphasis on realizing the value of our own family.

Q: So would you recommend other teachers to think about starting story-telling clubs at their schools?

A: Yes. I would say that the first thing to do is to tell stories yourself. You can't teach storytelling without telling stories. You can't understand the experience unless you try it yourself. Second, you don't have to be a theatre teacher. You don't have to have any knowledge of theatre. All you need is a knowledge of sequence and order. And you have to trust kids and pull yourself out of the picture as much as possible. I mean the traditional teaching mold is to be right up front controlling and directing, but you can't do that. The only other thing I'd say to teachers is that I know that time during the day is very limited. But storytelling leads to other uses. It can use history and creative writing. So it's never a "waste of time."

Epilogue

So, THIS is the book. If you have journeyed with us all the way through the book, you've learned reasons for telling stories, ideas about how to tell stories, and activities to help you find your own storytelling voice.

We leave you with a quote that is special to us—one that reminds us of the power of story.

> "I would ask you to remember only this one thing," said Badger. "The stories people tell have a way of taking care of them. If stories come to you, care for them. And learn to give them away where they are needed. Sometimes a person needs a story more than food to stay alive. That is why we put these stories in each other's memory. This is how people care for themselves."
>
> *Barry Lopez*

References and Resources

Storytelling is a form which reveals truths that reality obscures.

Jessamyn West

Print

Aardeman, V. 1994. *Misoso: Once Upon a Time Tales from Africa.* Westminster, MD: Random House.

Adell, J., and Klein, H. 1976. *A Guide to Nonsexist Children's Books.* Chicago: Academy Press.

Aipes, J., ed. 1994. *The Outspoken Princess and the Gentle Knight: A Treasury of Modern Fairy Tales.* New York: Bantam Books.

Akeret, R. 1991. *Family Tales, Family Wisdom.* New York: William Morrow and Company.

Allison, C. 1987. *I'll Tell You a Story, I'll Sing You a Song.* New York: Dell.

Allstrom, E. 1957. *Let's Play a Story.* New York: Friendship Press.

Baker, A., and Greene, E. 1977. *Storytelling: Art and Technique.* 2d ed. New York: R. R. Bowker.

Barton, B. 1986. *Tell Me Another.* Markham, Ontario: Pembroke Publishers.

Barton, B., and Booth, D. 1990. *Stories in the Classroom: Storytelling, Reading Aloud, and Roleplaying with Children.* Portsmouth, NH: Heinemann.

Bauer, C. 1977. *Handbook for Storytellers.* Chicago: American Language Association.

Bauer, C. 1993. *New Handbook for Storytellers.* New York: American Library Association.

Bauman, R. 1986. *Story, Performance and Event: Contextual Studies of Oral Narrative.* Cambridge: Cambridge University Press.

Berthoff, A. 1981. *The Making of Meaning: Metaphors, Models, and Maxims for Writing Teachers.* Montclair, NJ: Boynton/Cook.

Bettelheim, B. 1975. *The Uses of Enchantment.* New York: Vintage Books.

Blaustein, R. 1989. "A Guide to Collecting Family History and Community Traditions." *Brothers Grimm Newsletter* 2: 4–8.

Boras, R., Sheedy, J., and Siegel, M. 1990. "The Power of Stories in Learning Mathematics." *Language Arts* 67:174–188.

Boscov, R. 1985. "Storytellers." *Dramatics* 63:39–41.

Bosma, B. 1992. *Fairy Tales, Fables, Legends and Myths: Using Folk Literature in Your Classroom.* 2d ed. New York: Teachers College Press.

Brenemann, L., and Brenemann, B. 1983. *Once Upon a Time: A Storytelling Handbook.* Chicago: Nelson-Hall.

Brett, D. 1988. *Annie's Stories.* New York: Workman Publishing.

Briggs, N., and Wagner, J. 1979. *Children's Literature Through Storytelling and Drama.* Dubuque, IA: Wm. C. Brown.

Bruffee, K. 1980. *A Short Course in Writing.* 2d ed. Boston: Little, Brown.

_____. 1984. "Collaborative Learning and the Conversation of Mankind." *College English* 46: 637.

Bruner, J. 1986. *Actual Minds, Possible Worlds.* Cambridge, MA: Harvard University Press.

Bushnaq, I. 1986. *Arab Folktales.* New York: Pantheon.

Caduto, M., and Bruchac, J. 1988. *Keepers of the Earth.* Jonesborough, TN: National Association for the Preservation and Perpetuation of Storytelling.

Campbell, A. 1988. *The Power of Myth.* New York: Doubleday.

Carpenter, F. 1937. *Tales of a Chinese Grandmother.* New York: Doubleday.

Chalmers, A. 1973. *Introducing Books to Children.* London: Heinemann.

Clark, A. N. 1969. *Journey to the People.* New York: Viking.

Clark, E. C., Hyde, M., and McMahan, E. 1981. *"Developing Instruction in Oral History: A New Avenue for Speech Communication."* Communication Education 30: 238–244.

Cohan, S., and Shines, L. 1988. *Telling Stories: A Theoretical Analysis of Narrative Fiction.* New York: Routledge.

Cole, J. 1983. *Best Loved Folktales of the World.* New York: Doubleday.

Coles, R. 1989. *The Call of Stories: Teaching and the Moral Imagination.* Boston: Houghton Mifflin.

Cooper, P. 1988. *Looking into Classrooms: Storytelling as a Teaching Strategy.* Paper presented at annual meeting of Speech Communication Association, San Francisco.

_____. 1989. *Using Storytelling to Teach Oral Communication Competencies K–12.* Paper presented at annual meeting of Speech Communication Association, San Francisco.

_____. 1994. "Stories as Instructional Strategy: Teaching in Another Culture." *Basic Communication Course Annual* VI: 207–216.

_____. 1995. *Communication for the Classroom Teacher.* Scottsdale, AZ: Gorsuch Scarisbrick, Publishers.

Courlander, H. 1959. *The Tiger's Whisker and Other Tales: Legends from Asia and the Pacific.* New York: Harcourt Brace Jovanovich.

Cullum, A. 1971. *The Geranium on the Window Sill Just Died but Teacher, You Went Right On.* Holland: Harlon Quist.

Dailey, S. 1985. *Storytelling: A Creative Teaching Strategy.* Mt. Pleasant, MI: Storytime Productions. (Obtain by writing to Sheila Dailey, Box 2020, Mt. Pleasant, MI 48804-2020.)

_____. 1994. *Putting the World in a Nutshell: The Art of the Formula Tale.* New York: H. W. Wilson.

Denman, G. 1991. *Sit Tight, and I'll Swing You a Tail.* Portsmouth, NH: Heinemann.

Downs, V., Javidi, M., and Nussbaum, J. 1988. "An Analysis of Teachers' Verbal Communication Within the College Classroom: Use of Humor, Self-Disclosure, and Narratives." *Communication Education* 37: 127–141.

Fisher, A. 1984. "Narration as a Human Paradigm." *Communication Monographs* 51:1–22.

_____. 1989. *Human Communication as Narration: Toward a Philosophy of Reason, Value, and Action*. Columbia, SC: University of South Carolina Press.

Folklife Sourcebook: A Directory of Folklife Resources in the United States. Available from American Folklife Center, Superintendent of Documents, P.O. Box 371954, Pittsburgh, PA 15250-7954 (Include stock number S/N 030-001-00152-1.)

Fox, M. 1985. *Wilfrid Gordon McDonald Partridge*. New York: Kane/Miller.

Gee, J. P. 1986. "Orality and Literacy: From the Savage Mind to Ways with Words." *TESOL Quarterly* 20:719–745.

Greene, E., and Shannon, G. 1986. *Storytelling: A Selected Bibliography*. New York: Garland Publishing.

Griffin, B. *Storyteller Guidebook Series*. Medford, OR: Author. (Obtain by writing Barbara Griffin, 10 S. Keenaway Dr., Medford, OR 97504.)

Gross, A., and Batchelder, M. 1986. "Storytelling: A Process Approach to Speaking Skills." In S. M. Nugent (Ed.), *Integrating Speaking Skills into the Curriculum*. Boston: New England Association of Teachers of English.

Hamilton, V. 1969. *The Time-Ago Tales of Jahdu*. New York: Macmillan.

_____. 1992. *Many Thousand Gone: African Americans from Slavery to Freedom*. New York: Knopf.

Hamilton, M., and Weiss, M. 1990. *Children Tell Stories*. New York: Richard C. Owen.

Heilbrun, C. 1989. *Writing the Woman's Life*. New York: W. W. Norton.

Heinig, R. 1987. *Creative Drama Resource Book*. Englewood Cliffs, NJ: Prentice-Hall.

_____. 1992. Improvisation with Favorite Tales. Portsmouth, NH: Heinemann.

Holladay, S. J. 1987. *Narrative Activity and Teacher Effectiveness: An Investigation of the Nature of Storytelling in the Classroom*. Paper presented at annual meeting of Speech Communication Association, Boston.

Holmes, N. 1988. "We're All Storytellers." *Learning '88* 17:82–84.

Hutchinson, D. 1985. *Storytelling Tips*. Lincoln, NE: Foundation Books.

Kalmer, H. 1983. *Communication: Sharing Our Stories of Experience*. Seattle, WA: Psychological Press.

Kendall, F. 1983. *Diversity in the Classroom: A Multicultural Approach to Education of Young Children*. New York: Teachers College Press.

Kespek, M. 1990. "Telling Tales in School: A Revival of the Oral Tradition in the Nation's Classrooms." *Teacher* 1:30–33.

Kinghorn, H., and Pelton, M.H. 1991. *Every Child a Storyteller: A Handbook of Ideas*. New York: Teacher Ideas Press.

Kirkwood, W. 1983. "Storytelling and Self-Confrontation: Parables as Communication Strategies." *Quarterly Journal of Speech* 69:58–74.

Lakoff, G., and Johnson, M. 1980. *Metaphors We Live By*. Chicago: University of Chicago Press.

Lawson, A. 1987. *The Talking Bird and the Story Pouch*. New York: Harper and Row.

Lewis, R. 1979. "*As the twig is bent . . .*" *Parabola* 4:62–78.

Lipman, D. 1991. "Friendly Persuasion." *Storytelling* 8:13–18.

Livo, N., and Rietz, S. 1986. *Storytelling: Process and Practice*. Littleton, CO: Libraries Unlimited.

_____. 1987. *Storytelling Activities*. Littleton, CO: Libraries Unlimited.

MacDonald M. 1986. *Twenty Tellable Tales*. New York: H. W. Wilson Publishing.

_____. 1994. *A Parent's Guide to Storytelling*. New York: Harper Collins.

Maguire, J. 1985. *Creative Storytelling: Choosing, Inventing, and Sharing Tales for Children*. New York: McGraw-Hill.

_____. 1988. "Sounds and Sensibilities: Storytelling as an Educational Process." *Children's Literature Association Quarterly* 13:4–8.

Majors, R. 1989. *What Is Storytelling? The Theoretical Framework for Classroom Storytelling*. Paper presented at annual meeting of Speech Communication Association, San Francisco.

McAdams, D. P. 1993. *Stories We Live By: Personal Myths and the Making of the Self*. New York: William Morrow and Company.

McGill, A. 1988. *Flying Africans*. Jonesborough, TN: National Association for the Preservation and Perpetuation of Storytelling.

Medina, E. 1986. "Enhance Your Curriculum Through Storytelling." *Learning '86* 15:58–61.

Mikkelsen, N. 1984. "Literature and the Storymaking Power of Children." *Children's Literature Association Quarterly* 9:9–14.

Moore, R. 1991. *Awakening the Hidden Storyteller: How to Build a Storytelling Tradition in Your Family*. Springhouse, PA: Shambhala.

Moses, N. 1988. "*Telling Tales Pays Dividends, in Class*." Chicago Tribune, May 1, Section 9:3, 6–7.

National Council of Teachers of English. 1982. *Essentials of English*. Urbana, IL: National Council of Teachers of English.

Nell, V. 1988. *Lost in a Book: The Psychology of Reading for Pleasure*. New Haven, CT: Yale University Press.

Newman, F. 1980. *Mouthsounds*. New York: Workman.

Norton, C. S. 1989. *Life Metaphors: Stories of Ordinary Survival*. Carbondale: Southern Illinois University Press.

Nussbaum, J., Comadena, M., and Holladay, S. 1987. "Classroom Verbal Behavior of Highly Effective Teachers." *Journal of Thought* 22:73–80.

O'Callahan, J. 1985. *Master's Class in Storytelling*. Marshfield, MA: Vineyard Productions.

_____. 1991. Storytelling seminar taught at Northwestern University.

O'Keefe, V. 1986. *Affecting Critical Thinking Through Speech*. Urbana, IL: ERIC Clearinghouse on Reading and Communication Skills.

Paley, V. 1990. *The Boy Who Would Be a Helicopter*. Cambridge, MA: Harvard University Press.

Pellowski, A. 1977. *The World of Storytelling*. New York: Bowker.

_____. 1984. *The Story Vine*. New York: Macmillan.

Pellowski, A., and Sweel, L. 1987. *The Family Storytelling Handbook*. New York: Macmillan.

Regan, C., and Freeman, B. 1977. *Stories for the Telling*. (Order from The Folktellers, P.O. Box 2898, Asheville, NC 28802.)

Reinher, R. 1987. "Storytelling." *Teachers and Writers Magazine* 18:1–7.

Resnick, L., and Klopfer, L. 1988. *Toward the Thinking Curriculum: Current Cognitive Research*. Annandale, VA: Association for Supervision and Curriculum Development.

Roney, R. C. 1989. "Back to the Basics with Storytelling." *Reading Teacher* 42:520–523.

Rosen, H. 1986. "The Importance of Story." *Language Arts* 63:226–237.

Ross, R. 1972. *Storyteller*. Columbus, OH: Charles Merrill.

Rossman, R. "'Tell Me a Story' Curriculum Packers." (Order from Randi Rossman, IBM/Good Housekeeping Story Contest, 5000 Park St. North, St. Petersburg, FL 33709-9989.)

Rubright, L. *Rabbit's Tale and Other Native American Myths and Legends: An Interdisciplinary Curriculum Guide* and *Mike Fink: A Ring-Tailed Roarer: An Interdisciplinary Storytelling Unit*. Both of these resources are available from the author, 340 E. Jefferson, St. Louis, MO 63122.

_____. 1994. Storytelling seminar taught at Northwestern University.

de Saint-Exupéry, A. 1943. *The Little Prince*. New York: Harcourt, Brace & World.

Sarris, G. 1990. "Storytelling in the Classroom: Crossing Vexed Chasms." *College English* 52:169–185.

Sawyer, R. 1977. *The Way of the Storyteller*. New York: Penguin.

Schimmel, N. 1992. *Just Enough to Make a Story*. 2d ed. Berkeley, CA: Sisters' Choice Press.

Schoafsma, D. 1989. "Gilbert's and Dave's Stories: Narrative and Knowing." *English Journal* 78:89–91.

Schram, P. 1987. *Jewish Stories One Generation Tells Another*. Jonesborough, TN: National Association for the Preservation and Perpetuation of Storytelling.

Schwartz, M. 1987. "Connecting to Language Through Story." *Language Arts* 64:603–610.

Shannon, G. 1985. *Stories to Solve*. New York: Greenwillow Books.

Shedlock, M. 1951. *The Art of the Storyteller*. New York: Dover.

Sills, C. 1988. "Interactive Learning in the Composition Classroom." In J. Golub (Ed.), *Focus on Collaborative Learning*. Urbana, IL: National Council of Teachers of English.

Singer, I. B. 1978, 1984. *Stories for Children*. New York: Farrar, Straus, & Giroux.

Smith, J. N. 1988. *Homespun: Tales from America's Favorite Storytellers*. New York: Crown.

Speech Communication Association. 1993. *Speaking and Listening Competencies for High School Graduates.* Annandale, VA: Speech Communication Association.

Speech Communication Association. 1993. *Essential Speaking and Listening Skills for Elementary School Students.* Annandale, VA: Speech Communication Association.

Stone, E. 1988. *Black Sheep and Kissing Cousins: How Our Family Stories Shape Us.* New York: Penguin Books.

Tanner, F. 1987. *Basic Drama Projects,* 5th ed. Caldwell, ID: Clark Publishing.

Thompson Learning. 1994. *Tales Around the World* (10 series books). New York: Thompson Learning.

Verriour, P. 1990. "Storying and Storytelling in Drama." *Language Arts* 67:144–150.

Wagner, J. 1970. *Children's Literature Through Storytelling.* Dubuque, IA: Wm. C. Brown.

Ward, W. 1952. *Stories to Dramatize.* New Orleans: Anchorage Press.

Wason-Ellam, L. 1991. *Start with a Story.* Portsmouth, NH: Heinemann.

Weiner, H. 1986. "Collaborative Learning in the Classroom: A Guide to Evaluation." *College English* 48:55.

Wells, B. 1986. *The Meaning Makers.* Portsmouth, NH: Heinemann.

White, W. 1982. *Speaking in Stories: Resources for Christian Storytellers.* Minneapolis: Augsburg Publishing.

Whitworth, R. 1988. "Collaborative Learning and Other Disasters." In J. Golub (Ed.), *Focus on Collaborative Learning.* Urbana, IL: National Council of Teachers of English.

Wilms, D., and Cooper, I. 1987. *A Guide to Nonsexist Children's Books.* Chicago: Academy Press.

Yolen J. 1986. *Favorite Folktales from Around the World.* New York: Pantheon.

Zeitlin, S., Kotkin, A., and Baker, H. 1982. *Celebration of American Family Folklore.* New York: Pantheon.

Magazines and Periodicals

The Junior Storyteller. A quarterly periodical for ages 9–12. Write to: Storycraft Publishing, Vivian Dubrovin, P.O. Box 205, Masonville, CO 80541.

Language Arts. (Feb. 1990). Entire issue devoted to theme of "Stories and Meanings."

The National Storytelling Directory. Published each year by The National Storytelling Association, lists periodicals, storytellers, storytelling events, production companies, educational opportunities, and organizations. All are listed by state.

Parabola. Published quarterly by Society for the Study of Myth and Tradition. Write to: Parabola, G.P.O. Box 165, Brooklyn, NY 11202.

Storytelling Magazine. Published quarterly by National Storytelling Association. Write to NSA, P.O. Box 309, Jonesborough, TN 37659.

Storytelling Software

"All About Me," an interactive computer program that guides users (ages 6 and up) through the building of family trees and collecting of family stories. Contact Harper Collins Publishers, Advanced Media Group, 10 E. 53rd St., New York, NY. 10022-5299 or call 800-424-6234.

Catalogs of Nonprint Resources

Artana Productions
P.O. Box 1054
Marshfield, MA 02050

August House Publishers
P.O. Box 3223
Little Rock, AR 72203
501-372-5450

Design Video Communications
P.O. Box 30054
Indianapolis, IN 46230
(Rives Collins has a videotape, "Creative Drama and Improvisation," 1990.)

Gentle Wind
Songs and Stories for Children
Box 3103
Albany, NY 12203

High Windy Audio
P.O. Box 553
Fairview, NC 28730
704-628-1728

National Storytelling Association
P.O. Box 309
Jonesborough, TN 37659
(800) 525-4514

Yellow Moon Press
P.O. Box 381316
Cambridge, MA 02238
617-776-2230

Appendix A
Short Lists of Essentials for Good Stories and Storytellers

PERHAPS THE following lists reflect those elements that you find essential for a good story and a good storyteller.* If not, we invite you to generate your own lists.

Final prioritized list of ten factors considered essential for a good story

1. Be one the teller cares about, has been touched by, and feels a keen desire to share.
2. Be appropriate for the audience, time, and place.
3. Feel right, distinctive, strong—worth learning to tell.
4. Have emotional appeal, courage, love, laughter, excitement, sentiment.
5. Connect in some way with the human condition.
6. Evoke a strong response from both the listener and the teller.
7. Fit the teller's personality.
8. Have strength of language (of some beauty, force, or specificity).
9. Be authentic—faithful to the culture from which it came.
10. Have a strong beginning and a satisfying conclusion.

Final prioritized list of factors judged to be essential for the best storytellers

1. Love the story and enjoy sharing it.
2. Able to see story as it is being told.
3. Love and respect the audience.
4. Know which stories are right for them.
5. Able to impart a sense of spontaneity to the tale.
6. Have a sense of timing.
7. Have heart, soul, warmth.
8. Have imagination.
9. Know how to use language effectively.
10. Have good eye contact.

From Clarabel Tanner's study of fifty-six selected expert storytellers, as reported in *The National Storytelling Journal* 5:2 (Spring/Summer 1988): 36–38. Reprinted with permission.

Appendix B
Storytelling Resources on the Internet

STORYTELLING IS, of course, a low-tech art form. However, it finds itself in the midst of the high-tech world of the Internet. All you need is a computer and a modem to explore the riches of this ancient art form in its newest setting.

The STORYTELL mailing list

STORYTELL, sponsored by the School of Library and Information Studies at Texas Woman's University, is a forum for discussing storytelling. All persons interested in storytelling are invited to participate: professional storytellers, amateur storytellers, people concerned with the rich history of storytelling, people who enjoy listening to stories, and those who speculate about the place of storytelling in the 21st century. The list will promote collaboration among those interested in storytelling, reflecting diverse viewpoints from around the world. The list is a place for discussion of issues and interaction on topics of concern to the storytelling community. It can serve as a source for information on conferences, workshops, and events, or a place to ask (and answer) questions about derivations of stories, intellectual freedom concerns, or organization of storytelling events.

To subscribe, send e-mail to STORYTELL-REQUEST@venus.twu.edu. Your message should contain the following line:

subscribe [your first name] [your last name]

You will receive a confirming message from the listserver (the computer that reads such messages automatically, and adds or removes people from the mailing list) providing further information about the list, including how to temporarily or permanently unsubscribe.

alt.arts.storytelling

A Usenet Newsgroup, this is a free-flowing bulletin board discussion of storytelling and related issues. Storytellers, writers, librarians, and teachers frequent this group, sharing announcements about storytelling events and swapping insights about this folk art form.

LONG ISLAND
UNIVERSITY
LIBRARIES

Storytelling resources on the World Wide Web (WWW)

This is a home page of resources for storytellers and story lovers alike. Compiled by Sherri Johnson, the Web address is:

> http://www.cc.swarthmore.edu/~sjohnson/stories/

This page links storytelling resources on the Internet. As the Web continues to expand (exponentially!), the resources for storytellers are sure to grow. Already the impressive list of resources includes:

- Storyteller home pages with biographies and booking information
- Children's Stories
- Internet Public Library's Story Hour
- Read-along Stories: By the ERIC Clearinghouse on Reading, English, and Communication
- Stories by Children
- Aesop's Fables: From the Gutenberg Project Collection
- Grimm's Fairy Tales: From the Online Book Initiative
- Tales from Other Cultures
- Native American Stories

The storytelling home page

This wonderful resource was authored by storyteller/puppeteer Jim Maroon and is presented on the World Wide Web by the Tejas Storytelling Association. The web address is:

> http://users.aol.com/storypage

The goal of this resource is to be as comprehensive as possible. It contains hypertext links to:

- the best of STORYTELL and the STORYTELL archives
- a live chat room called the Swapping Ground where storytellers can visit and share stories electronically
- home pages of professional storytellers
- home pages of storytelling festivals
- home pages of storytelling organizations, including the National Storytelling Association
- articles on storytelling
- children's literature resources for storytellers
- puppetry resources

DISCARDED
FROM
LIU LIBRARIES